GYPSY MUSIC

The Reverb series looks at the connections between music, artists and performers, musical cultures and places. It explores how our cultural and historical understanding of times and places may help us to appreciate a wide variety of music, and vice versa.

reverb-series.co.uk
Series editor: John Scanlan

Already published

The Beatles in Hamburg
Ian Inglis

Brazilian Jive: From Samba to Bossa and Rap
David Treece

Easy Riders, Rolling Stones: On the Road in America, from Delta Blues to '70s Rock
John Scanlan

Gypsy Music: The Balkans and Beyond
Alan Ashton-Smith

Heroes: David Bowie and Berlin
Tobias Rüther

Jimi Hendrix: Soundscapes
Marie-Paule Macdonald

Neil Young: American Traveller
Martin Halliwell

Nick Drake: Dreaming England
Nathan Wiseman-Trowse

Remixology: Tracing the Dub Diaspora
Paul Sullivan

Sting: From Northern Skies to Fields of Gold
Paul Carr

Tango: Sex and Rhythm of the City
Mike Gonzalez and Marianella Yanes

Van Halen: Exuberant California, Zen Rock'n'roll
John Scanlan

GYPSY MUSIC

THE BALKANS AND BEYOND

ALAN ASHTON-SMITH

REAKTION BOOKS

For Juno

Published by Reaktion Books Ltd
Unit 32, Waterside
44–48 Wharf Road
London N1 7UX, UK
www.reaktionbooks.co.uk

First published 2017
Copyright © Alan Ashton-Smith 2017

Printed and bound in Great Britain by Bell & Bain, Glasgow

A catalogue record for this book is available from the British Library

ISBN 978 1 78023 823 4

CONTENTS

INTRODUCTION

> During the tempestuous finale of this performance it was as
> if every possible sound or tone was crushing down together
> like mountain crests which fall with a frightful uproar on
> sheets of sand mixed with blocks of rock and stone. We felt
> uncertain whether the edifice, which seemed to rock with
> these sudden displacements of sonorous currents and vibra-
> tions, would not really fall upon our heads; such was the
> crushing nature of the instrumentation of the concerto which
> all the conservatoires of the world would certainly have con-
> demned and even we found to be just a trifle risky.[1]

> Its oompah is revved up to thrash-metal speeds; bass lines
> from two tubas made the floor shake; its trumpets and saxo-
> phones raced through melodies like bullet trains taking hair-
> pin turns. It was brutally exhilarating.[2]

The first of the above passages is from Franz Liszt's *The Gipsy in
Music*, first published in 1859, and is a description of the farewell
concert given at the end of Liszt's visit to a Romani camp in
Hungary, a performance which took place in the shed of an inn
during a thunderstorm. The passage expresses the physicality and
the unpredictability of the style known as gypsy music, but it also
describes elements of danger and even immorality. A century and
a half later, gypsy music continues to be described in a similar
fashion, as is apparent in the second passage, a review of a 2014
performance by the Romanian Roma band Fanfare Ciocărlia.
The shaking floor recalls the 'sonorous currents and vibrations'
in Liszt's description; the hairpin turns in the second passage have
the same connotation of extremity as the mountain crests in the

first; and the thrash metal to which Fanfare Ciocărlia is compared is no doubt subject to the disdain, if not the condemnation, of the world's conservatoires.

When gypsy music is described it is often with the use of tropes that have endured for centuries. This might suggest a homogeneous genre, slow to evolve, and with a firmly fixed canon. But the opposite is in fact true. Duelling violins, plaintive accordions, intricately picked guitars and blaring horns are all associated with gypsy music, but each of these moods and each of these instruments sounds quite different from the others. Indeed, the differences are in some ways so substantial that it is perhaps not realistic to describe gypsy music within the framework of a genre. Yet there is something almost imperceptible that ties these and many other sounds together, with the result that they are all described as gypsy.

Defining what gypsy music actually is, therefore, is not straightforward. Nevertheless, that is what I seek to do in this book, and the means by which I do so is an examination of the connections between gypsy music and the Balkans. The connections between gypsy music and specific places – including but by no means limited to the Balkans – constitute just one facet of the associations that have made gypsy music such a broad-ranging, and consequently such an ill-defined, category. In fact, this poor definition is not limited to gypsy music but also extends to the figure of the gypsy, which in the popular imagination is a mélange of contradictions and enigmas. Why, then, am I using place to define gypsy music?

Firstly, because the gypsy is an Other – perhaps the ultimate Other – and Otherness invites geographical definition. The process of Othering entails the assignation of the role of Other to a community so as to assert the dominance of the group that allots that role and to vilify the group cast as Other. Othering is important in studies of imperialism and post-colonialism

– amongst many more fields – and often comes about in a geographical context: for example, Edward Said notes in the introduction to *Orientalism* that the Orient is one of Europe's 'deepest and most recurring images of the Other'.[3] Orientalism is a classic form of Othering, but the Othering of the Roma is not typical in that it has no specific geographical context, and this is precisely because the Roma are not seen as having strong connections to places. To identify such connections is therefore to go beyond the trope of Otherness and to see the Roma and their music in a more rounded way.

Secondly, because the key locus of what is thought of as gypsy music is the Balkans, and 'Balkan' is just as poorly defined a concept as 'gypsy'. To describe something, or someone, as Balkan is to Other it just as it, or they, might be Othered in being described as gypsy. There are strong correlations between gypsy music and the idea of the Balkans and, as we shall see, these correlations are dependent on the process of Othering.

Finally, because the gypsy figure is traditionally and stereo-typically nomadic. Although most Roma are now settled, the notion of the 'wandering gypsy' remains prevalent in the popular imagination. In order to define a figure that is seen as being dissociated from fixed locations it is perhaps most productive to seek out any links to places that do exist. Similarly, to define gypsy music, which is globally recognized and which has travelled the world in many incarnations and guises, it is sensible to identify where strong links to places can be made. In the case of the gypsy, and indeed in the case of gypsy music, it is in the Balkans that links to places are most comfortably and readily made.

However, these links are certainly not limited to the Balkans, so it is also necessary to go beyond the Balkans in order to define gypsy music. I begin this book by approaching gypsy music through reference to the Balkans as a possible origin point and as the locus in which gypsy music took on the forms in which it remains most widely recognizable today. I commence with an overview of the history of the Romani people, which will reveal how the association between the Romani people and music, and the association between gypsy music and the Balkans, came about. I then step a little beyond the Balkans to Hungary, to address how gypsy music was first formally defined outside of the Balkans, and the ensuing debates about how it should be understood. Franz Liszt asserted that all Hungarian music was derived from the music of the Roma; his critics, including Béla Bartók, claimed that the music often regarded as gypsy music is in fact not intrinsic to the Romani people. I then return to the Balkans to discuss how negative portrayals of the region might have informed perceptions of the Roma and of gypsy music, and subsequently I review contemporary gypsy music in the Balkans by considering three bands who together illuminate the range of styles played in the region and exported to listeners outside it.

I then go on to consider gypsy music more widely by exploring some of the forms it has mutated and hybridized into outside of the Balkans – although it will become apparent that such mutation and hybridization has also occurred within the Balkans. In the latter part of the book I will consider four styles of music that are thought of as gypsy but which came about in distinct parts of Europe and which are also the result of other influences.

I begin with Russian gypsy music, seeking to establish connections with the styles of gypsy music previously considered. I then move to Western Europe – first to Spain and flamenco, which is typically seen as a gypsy music, but which in fact has wider roots. Flamenco is also associated with the *gitano*. Perceptions of this figure are somewhat different to those of the gypsy figure, and I will also examine this difference, and the fact that there are other terms of definition connected to, yet separate from, the gypsy. My next case study is gypsy jazz.

The best-known player of this genre is its founding father, Django Reinhardt, and although he was a Romani musician, gypsy jazz remains a subgenre of jazz as much as it is one of gypsy music. Here, I will assess the extent to which gypsy jazz has been consumed as a gypsy music and as a hybrid.

Finally, I will examine two more recently developed styles of gypsy music: gypsy punk and Balkan beats. The first of these is, as its name suggests, a hybrid of punk foundations and gypsy music accents, while the latter is a form of electronic music that often involves the sampling and remixing of traditional gypsy music. However, the musicians who play these styles are almost exclusively non-Roma, so the degree to which they should be regarded as gypsy music is open to debate. It is clear that gypsy music has constantly evolved, and it is likely that its parameters, and thus its definition, have shifted over time.

Before we proceed any further, however, we must consider the key concepts that we are dealing with: 'gypsy' and 'Balkan'. These are at the core of this book, and interlock not only because both have been Othered, but also because the Balkans has the largest concentrations of Romani people in the world, and is the origin point of much of the gypsy music consumed by global audiences today. I deliberately describe both as concepts in some detail because, as we shall see, they signify so much more than their obvious definitions.

Before we can consider the cultural connotations of 'Balkan', we should establish its geographic parameters, as there have been many views on which countries and areas may be considered to be part of the Balkans. The only entirely constant constituents are Bulgaria and Albania. Yugoslavia was also described unanimously as Balkan, but since that country broke up into separate states in the early 1990s there have been deviations. Slovenia, which lies at the northwestern corner of the Balkans, is often omitted, and Croatia has also been exempted by some commentators.[4] Romania is almost always regarded as Balkan, but Moldova, its neighbour to the east, is often thought to be beyond the region's outer reaches.

Although Turkey is primarily situated outside of Europe, and thus cannot wholly be part of the Balkans, the part of the Marmara region that is within Europe is generally included. This acknowledges the influence of Ottoman rule on much of the Balkans; from the fifteenth century until the early twentieth century the region was largely part of the Ottoman Empire. It is also significant that the word 'Balkan', which originally described a mountain range in Bulgaria, is of Ottoman origin. Greece is included within the Balkans more often than not, but since it was not part of the Ottoman Empire and was never a socialist state, it is sometimes excluded. The great civilization associated with Attic Greece also conflicts with the stereotype of barbarity that is attributed to the Balkans, another reason for Greece's omission by some.[5] It should also be noted that the various historical maps of the Balkans that appear in many books on the subject suggest that the region may have, or at least has had, borders that do not correspond with any current national borders. For example, Misha Glenny's survey opens with a map entitled 'The Balkans, 1804', which includes parts of, though not all of, present-day Romania and Serbia.

My own mapping, which is intended as a way of understanding the meaning of 'Balkan' in a musical context, follows the precedent of leaving Greece outside of the Balkans, for the reasons already outlined. In addition, since Greece has long been a popular destination for Western tourists, it does not have the unknown or Other quality of the rest of the region – nor does it have as substantial a Romani population as most of the countries I include. I also omit Turkey: although the Ottoman Empire undoubtedly shaped the Balkans and existing perceptions of

Map of the Balkans.

the area, the fact that it was the controlling power in the region makes it very different from the other Balkan countries. The current perceptions of the Balkans that I will go on to examine are largely based on their quasi-colonial status, and this status cannot be applied to Turkey. However, I include all of the formerly Yugoslavian countries, since their Yugoslav histories inform the way that they are perceived. I also include Romania and Moldova, along with Bulgaria and Albania.

Just as we need to understand the parameters of the Balkan region before considering their connotations of 'Balkan', it is necessary to define the gypsy before we can define gypsy music. This might appear to be an obvious point, and 'gypsy' may at first seem very easy to define, but it is in fact a loaded term; the figure of the gypsy is an ambiguous one with a fraught and complex history. Foremost, it is important to distinguish between the Romani people and the figure of the gypsy; there are many falsehoods about the Roma that have been perpetuated as if they were fact, and these have informed perceptions about the gypsy figure and about gypsy music. Moreover, the gypsy has become as much an idea as an actual figure, 'meaningful as a sign precisely because it resists definition yet contains within itself certain associations'.[6]

A review of previous attempts at defining 'gypsy' suggests that it is easier to identify what the word does not stand for than what it does. This is in part due to the fact that 'gypsy' does not refer to a single group: peoples with different languages, cultures and racial identities are described as 'gypsy', and there is a sense that these peoples cannot easily be distinguished from one another.[7] The writer Ian Hancock, who identifies himself as Romani, argues that even from the perspective of the Romani people, this is to some degree the case, and informs their self-identification. He states that:

any sense of having once been a single people has long been lost, the common factor now being an awareness not of what we *are*, but of what all of us are *not*. Romanies are not *gadže* or non-Romani people.[8]

It is important that the Romani people are acknowledged as being contributors to what is understood by 'gypsy'. While it is the case that those outside the Romani community, including governments, academics and the general population, inform the definition, these groups are more likely to engage in Othering, whether or not they do so consciously.[9] With numerous stakeholders involved, there is potential for considerable discrepancies between definitions of the gypsy, and the task is made more complex still when we consider the range of peoples who are referred to as gypsies.

This encompasses groups of Roma with their own ethnic designations, including *gitanos* in Spain, *Sinti* in Germany and Central Europe, *Kalderash* in Romania, and *Manouches* in France. In the context of the UK and Ireland, we find that Travellers who are not necessarily of Romani descent, primarily Irish Travellers, are also commonly referred to as gypsies.[10] Complicating things further still, there is a school of thought (to which Hancock belongs) that shuns the idea of distinct groups and which regards many of these various appellations as being incorrectly applied names used by non-Roma. There are of course local names equivalent to the English word 'gypsy', such as *cigan* in Slavic languages and *Zigeuner* in German, and there is a risk that these designations used by non-Roma may become confused with the terms that Romani people use to describe themselves.

Hancock insists on the use of the term 'Romani', declaring that 'other depictions with other names are misleading, and sometimes even harmful.'[11] He continues with the statement that 'we all call ourselves Romani', which is not strictly true since, while some Roma find 'gypsy' an offensive slur, others use it to refer to themselves. His point that the Roma have two identities, one an actual Romani identity and the other the one understood by non-Roma, is an excellent one.[12] However, we should remember that it is perhaps rather tenuous claims about what defines the Romani people that have led to their being simultaneously vilified and romanticized. Importantly, Hancock acknowledges that there are differences between the Romani peoples who live in different regions of Europe – and this is a distinction that we might expect to find paralleled in gypsy music.

Reliable information about the Roma can be difficult to find, and this further explains why non-Roma have perpetuated inaccuracies. Although the Romani people are a substantial global minority group, estimates of their exact populations vary significantly. This is due to a lack of official census data; many Roma are not recorded on censuses and many more choose not to declare that they are Roma. The Council of Europe estimates that there are between ten and twelve million Roma in Europe alone; even if this is an overestimation, we can conclude from more conservative estimates related to individual countries worldwide that there are certainly at least that many Roma globally.[13] There are Romani communities all over the world, but their largest populations are in Europe. France, Spain and Italy all have very substantial populations, but Eastern European and Balkan countries, particularly Hungary, Slovakia, Romania, Bulgaria, Serbia and Macedonia, have the largest concentrations of Romani people.

Since they are widely dispersed and have no designated homeland or nation state, and since many Roma have lived nomadic lifestyles, they are often disassociated from particular places. Speculation about their origins as a race, and lack of knowledge regarding their history, has led to them being thought of as a people without a past. These perceptions can be found not only in popular discourse, but also in some scholarly works. 'History has been an alien concept in Romani culture,' says Zoltan Barany, 'where the dead are rarely mentioned and seldom become the subjects of commemoration.'[14] Alaina Lemon has noted that 'Gypsies are usually depicted not only as people "without history" but as indifferent to recollection, living in an "eternal present".'[15] But 'Roma nevertheless are and speak of themselves as connected to local places and pasts.'[16] They are also connected to a single, unifying past.

Although the Roma have always fascinated outside observers, who have been curious about their origins and way of life, the way that their culture has been received by non-Roma reveals a marked dichotomy. The idea of the gypsy has two sides, and the use of the word 'gypsy' suggests a stereotype with connotations that face in quite different directions. On one side, there is the romanticized, exoticized idea of the gypsy that is suggestive of mystique and magic; on the other the pariah figure associated with crime and dirt.[17]

Certain cultural aspects, particularly music, dress and folklore, have long been attractive to the nationals of every country that has a Romani population. However, other aspects, such as notions of hygiene and cleanliness, and attitudes to work and money, are typically regarded with disdain. The Roma have thus been simultaneously romanticized and vilified, their music, dress and certain of their traditions admired while many other aspects of their lifestyles are reviled. Perceptions are often exoticized and tend to go hand in hand with discrimination.

These perceptions continue to be perpetuated, but in order to show how deeply entrenched they are it is worth considering the gypsy in some of the many fictional texts from the nineteenth century and earlier that present Romani characters. Gypsies can be found in many literary works, and the particular appeal that the gypsy figure has had for writers can perhaps be attributed to the dual stereotype attached to it, which can be manipulated for dramatic and narrative purposes.[18] The figure of the gypsy has been presented in a very similar way throughout Europe; 'reduced to a textual effect' rather than being permitted a representative history.[19] As we shall see, the Roma are misrepresented by such portrayals, which have come to inform continuing perceptions more strongly than accurate studies. One particularly well-known example of a gypsy figure is the character of Heathcliff in Emily Brontë's *Wuthering Heights* (1847), who is thought of as an archetypal Romantic hero. Although his origins are unknown, since he was found as an infant on the streets of Liverpool, the first impression of him that is shared with readers is that:

> He is a dark skinned gypsy, in aspect, in dress, and manners a gentleman, that is as much a gentleman as many a country squire: rather slovenly, perhaps, yet not looking amiss with his negligence, because he has an erect and handsome figure, and rather morose.[20]

Whether or not Brontë intended Heathcliff to be a Rom, she portrays him as a gypsy not only in his physical appearance – dark, attractive but somewhat unkempt – but also in his character: he is passionate yet savage and ultimately unknowable.

While *Wuthering Heights* is the best-known text from this period that presents a gypsy figure, the most detailed characterizations of gypsies can be found in the work of the linguist George Borrow, who had a lifelong interest in them. His autobiographical novel *Lavengro* (1851) and its sequel *The Romany Rye* (1857) provide an account of Borrow's youth, devoting a considerable portion of the narrative to this fascination. This is connected to his interest in linguistics (Borrow learned many languages, and *lavengro* is the Romani word for 'linguist'), and his ability to communicate with Romani people in their own tongue is presented as an important part of his good relations with them.

Although Borrow produced some accurate accounts of Romani life in both England and Spain, and a Romani dictionary, *Romano Lavo-lil*, his presentation of the Roma in *Lavengro* conforms to the typical exoticized view. His primary gypsy character, Jasper Petulengro, is a gambling, horse-dealing, fist-fighting nomad who only works out of strict economic necessity. The other main gypsy figure is Mrs Hearne, a short-tempered woman who decamps to Yorkshire after a row with Borrow. When he re-encounters her she feeds him a poisoned cake; thereafter there are numerous references to poisoning or 'drubbing' pigs, a dishonest means of obtaining food that is employed frequently by Borrow's gypsies. Borrow uses the Romani language to describe this process, and this gives the act of deception a sense of mystery that forms part of the unknowable quality of gypsies.

Borrow adopted an itinerant lifestyle in an attempt to better understand and empathize with his Romani subjects. It is likely that this was a very deliberate move, but in his novels he presents it as though it was a state he fell into quite naturally. Having struggled to earn a living in London by writing, he leaves the city as soon as he has managed to sell a book; subsequently he travels indiscriminately from place to place. After some time he buys a wagon from a disheartened tinker and takes to the road. When he describes his attempts at taking up the tinker's trade, he writes in a mixture of English and Romani. While attempting to pass as a gypsy, he encounters a priest who is unconvinced and correctly guesses that he has simply adopted a gypsy lifestyle. Borrow is reluctant to admit that he is not a gypsy, as this would de-mythologize his way of life. While it is considered acceptable, and even romantic, for a gypsy to be without fixed home or occupation, the romanticized view of an untamed figure living freely as a nomad does not compensate for the vilification to which the Roma are habitually subjected. A non-Roma who adopts this kind of lifestyle acquires gypsy associations, but gains none of the exotic qualities assigned to this figure, and is thus an object of disdain.

The kind of fascination with the Roma that led to such fictional representations was of course not confined to writing in English.[21] Amongst the earliest examples is Cervantes's novel *La Gitanilla* (The Little Gypsy Girl, 1613). This text begins with the following description, which proves how enduring the association between gypsies and theft has been: 'It should seem that the race of Gypsies, male and female, are only born into the world to be thieves; their parents are thieves, they are bred up thieves, they study thieving.'[22] It is also significant that the central character, who is distinguished from the other gypsies on account of her beauty, musical talent and ability to read and write, is in fact a non-Roma who was stolen by gypsies as an infant. Two centuries later, the French writer Prosper Mérimée's novella *Carmen* (1845), which was the source for Bizet's famous opera, introduced another well-known gypsy character.[23] If Heathcliff is an archetypal male romantic hero, then Carmen serves as a female counterpart. In this text, we find Mérimée travelling in Spain, where he encounters his heroine. In their first exchange, he attempts to determine where she is from, first guessing Córdoba or Andalucía, then that she is from the Middle East, or Moorish. Carmen replies that she is in fact 'bohémienne' – a gypsy.[24] Like Heathcliff, she is strikingly attractive; her beauty is described as 'strange and savage'.[25] Carmen is initially presented as a fortune-teller; we later learn that she was an outlaw who married a man on the run; when she leaves him for another man, he stabs her to death. Confessing his murder, he says that it is the Roma who are ultimately to blame, for the way in which they raised Carmen.[26]

As she is killed, Carmen declares that she 'will always be free'.[27] This is a desire that is often associated with the gypsy;

John Thomas Borrow, *George Borrow*, c. 1821–4, oil on canvas.

a similar reference can be found in Alexander Pushkin's narrative poem 'The Gypsies' (1824). This text in fact has a similar plot to *Carmen*; a young man named Aleko falls in love with a Romani girl, Zemfira; when she leaves him for another man, he murders her and her new lover. The notion that she, like all gypsies, must be free, is reiterated throughout 'The Gypsies'; indeed, this is apparent from the very start of the poem:

> Like freedom their encampment feels
> Joyful, their sleep beneath the skies
> Carefree; among the wagon-wheels,
> Half-covered with scant canopies,
> Fires burn, with families intent
> Upon their supper; on the lea
> The horses graze; behind one tent
> A bear lies fast asleep and free.[28]

In addition to the concern with freedom that can be observed here, there are numerous other features characteristic of depictions of gypsies: the campfire, the 'scant canopies' suggestive of limited resources, and the dancing bear that provides a source of income. We may also detect a precedent for Borrow's writing here, in the character of Aleko, who joins a Romani caravan. The trope of a non-Roma, often an outlaw, living amongst the gypsies can frequently be observed in texts that centre around gypsy characters. In Pushkin's poem, Zemfira introduces Aleko to her father, and explains his situation:

> 'Father,' declares the girl, 'I found
> A guest out there, beside a mound;
> I've asked him home to stay with us.
> He wants to be a gypsy too;
> The law is after him, he says,
> But I shall be his love and true . . .'[29]

In a highly romanticized rendering of Romani culture, Pushkin has the old man accept this arrangement without question, and invite Aleko to take up a traditional gypsy occupation:

> Be one of us, and live our life –
> The threadbare freedom of the road.

We're off tomorrow with our load;
Choose a trade to suit your flair,
Blacksmith, singer, or the bear.[30]

The overarching suggestion of 'The Gypsies' is that it is easy
to become a gypsy and that in doing so one can lead a carefree
lifestyle. Another figure who attempted to 'become' a gypsy
in this way was the artist Augustus John. The gypsy has long
been a figure commonly portrayed by artists; several of David
Teniers the Younger's landscapes, for example, featured gypsy
figures, presumably to enhance their sense of wildness and add
emotional resonance. However, John's lifelong fascination with
the Roma extended beyond his art. In common with Borrow,
he had an interest in the Romani language – a product of his
friendship with John Sampson, who was writing a book about the
language, entitled *The Dialect of the Gypsies of Wales*.[31] Eventually,
John was to become so immersed in the image of the gypsy that
he fabricated a heritage for himself.[32] Although he pursued his
fascination so far as to purchase a traditional Romani wagon and
horse, in which he travelled with his family for some time, the
death of his wife in 1907 persuaded him to abandon the nomadic
lifestyle. Presumably the reality of living on the road was less
appealing than the romantic gypsy stereotype. George Borrow's
nomadic period was also short-term, adding up to no more than
three months in total.[33]

Popular texts like *Wuthering Heights* and *Carmen* continue
to be consumed today, and the image of the gypsy they present
barely differs from the contemporary gypsy figure. The way that
the Romani people are portrayed in the media and in textual
representations generally retains characteristics such as the desire
for freedom, exotic beauty, dishonesty and savagery. References
to gypsy fashion are more common than reports of the issues
facing Romani people; the consensus seems to be that the reality

David Teniers the Younger, *Gypsies in a Landscape*, before 1690, oil on panel.

of being Romani is far less interesting and attractive than the mythology of the gypsy.

The image has also been perpetuated in popular music that has no connection to the Romani people or their music. The gypsy figure appears frequently in British and Irish folk music, for example. Just two of many instances can be found in the songs 'The Raggle Taggle Gypsy' and 'The Whistling Gypsy', worth mentioning here because both tell the tales of wealthy ladies who leave their lives and lords to run off with a band of gypsies. This has clear parallels with Pushkin's poem, and with the lifestyle experiments of Borrow and John, and demonstrates the universality of the romantic notion that one can find greater freedom by taking up a gypsy lifestyle.

The gypsy image has also been deployed in other popular music genres. Jimi Hendrix called his post-Jimi Hendrix Experience group, and their 1970 album, Band of Gypsys, a name that plays on the romantic notion of the gypsy lifestyle and the long-standing association between the Roma and music. 'We're calling it the Band of Gypsys, because that's what we are,' Hendrix said. 'That's what all musicians are. The whole world is their front porch.'[34] The claim illustrates the universality of the gypsy image, and the fact that gypsiness is seen by many as a condition or lifestyle that can easily be adopted.

The range of popular music genres in which gypsy references can be found also demonstrates this universality. In the soft rock of Fleetwood Mac's 'Gypsy', the folk rock of Cher's 'Gypsys, Tramps and Thieves' and the heavy metal of Dio's 'Gypsy', the gypsy has symbolized freedom and mystery. This appropriation of the gypsy image has not been confined to pop and rock: Hungarian jazz guitarist Gábor Szabó, who was based in the USA for most of his career, also wrote a song called 'Gypsy Queen', which was subsequently covered by Carlos Santana: on one hand this references the gypsy jazz genre, and the Hungarian Romani music that influenced Szabó, but the title also functions as a hook with which to lure in listeners attracted by the gypsy stereotype and a belief that music and the gypsy figure intrinsically go together.

A reaction to these stereotypes appearing in music and literature has yet to occur. While some Roma rights activists have attempted to de-mythologize the Roma and reclaim their culture, setting out the elements that are correct and placing them within their proper context, there remains much work to be done. Accurate textual portrayals that might serve to rectify earlier misrepresentations are few in number, but are starting to appear more frequently. Amongst the more widely circulated examples are Alexander Ramati's *And the Violins Stopped Playing* (1985) and Ronald Lee's *Goddam Gypsy* (1971).

Although accounts written by Romani people are now more widely available, they remain far less accessible in the West than texts by non-Roma. As we have seen, there is a lengthy history of misrepresentation that has been perpetuated in part by textual portrayals. More recently, there have been numerous studies and ethnographies that attempt to provide a more accurate representation of the Roma. However, some of the more popular texts are not without their flaws; there is in particular a tendency towards generalization, with some authors ascribing qualities they have observed in certain Romani people or groups to all Roma.

An example is Isabel Fonseca's book *Bury Me Standing* (1995), a study of Romani culture based on her encounters with Roma throughout Eastern Europe. While she focuses on the realities, rather than being drawn to music and magic, Fonseca does have a tendency to generalize, stating, for instance, that 'Gypsies lie. They lie a lot – more often and more inventively than other people.'[35] Garth Cartwright's *Princes Amongst Men* (2005) is a comparable text, although it is specifically concerned with Romani musicians. Cartwright does aim to keep stereotyping and exoticism to a minimum, and his book is a useful source on Romani music, but there is nonetheless a degree of romanticism. In the opening chapter, for example, he writes: 'Gypsies. Fire. Like bread and butter, politicians and lies, you sense they instinctively go together.'[36] In addition, the fact that the heart of the book's subject-matter is music poses a problem. Music is a crucial part of the gypsy figure beloved of non-Roma, and therefore any accounts of Roma who play music risk perpetuating that stereotype. By beginning my exploration of gypsy music with a history of the Romani people I hope to avoid doing so here.

1 THE ORIGINS OF BALKAN GYPSY MUSIC

It is important to distinguish between the words 'gypsy' and 'Roma'. Although the two are often used interchangeably, they have very different connotations, and for my purposes in attempting to define gypsy music they have quite different meanings. Gypsy is considered by many to be a derogatory term – despite the fact that many Roma self-identify as such – and it is associated with wandering, criminality and the other stereotypes that we have already discussed. Roma is a less loaded term and its use helps to avoid the perpetuation of stereotyping.

As I continue to consider what gypsy music is, I will use the words 'Roma' and 'Romani' when referring to the Romani people, and the word 'gypsy' to signify the mythologized, exoticized construction of the Roma that often appears in non-Romani representation. I will refer to Romani music when describing the music played by Romani musicians, but the question at the heart of this book concerns gypsy music, and I will continue to use this term so as to acknowledge that this music has also in many cases been the product of exoticism and reconstruction by outsiders. As we shall see, some music can be described as both Romani music and gypsy music, but gypsy music is not always played by Romani people.

However, our investigation into gypsy music begins with the history of the Roma, which will illuminate how the Romani people became so strongly connected to and associated with music. It is generally agreed, based on linguistic and genetic evidence, that the origins of the Roma lie in Rajasthan, in northwestern India, and that they gradually migrated westwards and became dispersed. The motive for their initial migration from India is uncertain, but numerous suggestions have been made. Romani scholar Ian Hancock has posited that the Roma were a warrior caste, who were engaged in fighting the Muslim Ghaznavid Empire, which repeatedly invaded India during the eleventh century.[1] He believes that they began as an assembly of non-Aryans, who were considered by the Aryan castes to be expendable in battle, and accordingly were sent to the front line. As this army fought the invaders, they gradually took a westerly trajectory, and commenced their migration in this way. Ronald Lee dates the beginning of the diaspora to the same period, but goes a step further. His theory is that some of the Indian troops defeated by the Muslims were incorporated into the Ghaznavid army, and then became involved in raids in regions further east, such as Armenia. Displaced from India, this group of captive refugees eventually began to take on an identity that differentiated them from both their conquerors and their ancestors.[2]

However their diaspora began, it is indisputable that having moved gradually west through Persia and the Middle East, many Roma arrived in the Balkans, where large Romani populations continue to live. Hancock dates their first appearance in Europe to the end of the thirteenth century; there were certainly Roma in Europe shortly after this time, many of whom were enslaved.[3] This seems to have begun almost as soon as they appeared in the Balkans: Angus Fraser asserts that 'the first mention of Gypsies in Rumanian archives occurs in a document issued in 1385 . . . [which] . . . confirmed the grant of 40 families of Gypsies,' while Hancock cites references to Romani slaves that date back to earlier than 1355.[4] Meanwhile, David Crowe stresses that the widespread slavery of the Roma that occurred for centuries in parts of what is now Romania set the precedent for that country's particularly poor record of Roma integration, which persists to this day.[5] Although not all Roma were enslaved, persecution was universal. They were not permitted to lead the nomadic lifestyles that many had adopted, and were often subjected to unfair trials. Although the murder of Roma was not officially permitted, it was rarely punished. Fraser has written,

> Had all the anti-Gypsy laws which sprang up been enforced uncompromisingly, even for a few months, the Gypsies would have been eradicated from most of Christian Europe well before the middle of the sixteenth century.[6]

It was not until 1864, shortly after Lincoln's Emancipation Proclamation in the United States, that Romani slaves in the Balkans gained 'complete legal freedom'.[7] This period of slavery is a lengthy antecedent to a trend of persecution that continues to the present day. Regarded as savage intruders with unknown origins, the Roma have been reviled and subjected to severe discrimination.

This reached its nadir in the Holocaust perpetrated by Nazi Germany, a major manifestation of the persecution of the Roma that is often overlooked. Although numerous historians and scholars of Romani studies have begun to comment on the lack of attention that the Holocaust's Romani victims have received, and attempts to rectify this deficiency have lately been made, the loss of Romani life that occurred is more often than not still treated as a footnote to the mass extermination of the Jews.

While it is impossible to determine how many Roma died in the Holocaust – this is compounded by the unreliable data concerning their population – Hancock estimates that 'over half of the Romani population in Nazi-occupied Europe' was killed.[8] As Barany points out, 'The extermination of the Gypsies

Deportation of German Roma, 1940.

was far less meticulously documented by the Nazis and their collaborators than was the murder of the Jews,' and the Roma themselves, being largely illiterate, were less able to record their ordeal in writing.[9] The latter of these problems has persisted long after the end of the Third Reich: while many Jewish survivors have written accounts of the Holocaust, fewer Roma have been able to do so. An attempt towards countering this was made around 1971, when lyrics were composed for the traditional song 'Djelem Djelem' and it was adopted as a Romani anthem; these lyrics directly referenced the deaths of Roma in the Holocaust.

Countless versions of 'Djelem Djelem' have been recorded, from Šaban Bajramović's piano ballad interpretation to the version by the Antwerp Gipsy-Ska Orkestra, which recalls New Orleans funeral jazz, and the brass rendition of the Kočani Orkestar. But it is the more downbeat interpretations, such as Bajramović's, and Ljiljana Buttler's soulful recording, that really capture the spirit of the song's lyrics and the legacy of the Romani Holocaust. Survivors remain marginalized by governments, receiving substantially fewer reparations than their Jewish counterparts and encountering a resistance towards Romani Holocaust memorials. A programme of compensation for Jewish victims was established, but this was not the case for Romani victims.[10]

Systematic extermination of this kind is undoubtedly as severe as persecution of any race or group can be, but the end of the Second World War nonetheless brought a fresh form of oppression for the Roma. With most of Eastern Europe now under communist rule, the Roma who lived there were expected to conform to the expectations of this system. Accordingly, they were required to integrate, and any outward display of their particular culture, including music, was generally forbidden. In many cases being Romani was simply not permitted, and Roma were expected to define themselves as, for example, Bulgarian or Yugoslavian. This forced identity is one reason for a lack of reliable census data by which Romani populations might be measured today. Many Eastern European Roma now pine for the greater stability and socialist public services that they were afforded during the socialist era, and while many were better off in socio-economic terms, it was at the expense of their distinct identity.

It was not only identity that was revoked; many Roma in Eastern Europe also lost their mobility due to communist policy concerning nomadism.[11] This was not a particularly novel practice; almost since their first arrival in Eastern Europe Roma have been encouraged to settle, often in order that they could be taxed or enslaved. Maria Theresa, ruler of the Habsburg Empire from 1740 to 1780, passed a number of decrees aimed at removing the ethnic identity of the Roma so that they might be incorporated into the Hungarian race.[12] Although these were not fully enforced they will have contributed towards bringing the roaming of the Roma to a halt.

This drive towards forcing them into settlement was finalized under communism two hundred years later; attempts were made throughout the communist-controlled countries of Eastern Europe to assimilate the Roma as far as possible. This was often an aggressive process: in Poland, for example, wheels were removed from caravans and horses were shot.[13] Active initiatives towards assimilation began soon after the end of the Second World War: the majority of Romanian Roma were settled by the early 1950s, and most other countries were not far behind.[14] The levers used to drive settlement varied from offers of accommodation and employment to outright bans on movement. With the traditionally wandering Roma settled, they could be controlled more easily. In addition, animosity towards them meant that there was a desire to present them as being fewer in number than they actually were. Since there is a popular conflation of gypsy culture and nomadic lifestyles, it was their nomadism as much as anything else that marked the Roma out as gypsies, so rescinding this was seen as a way of revoking their identity.

The situation of Roma today is a product of this oppression. Throughout Europe, the majority are now sedentary and many live in ghettoized camps in poor conditions. Poverty is ubiquitous and unemployment levels are extremely high. Integration with the wider community is minimal and persecution is rife. In many countries there is no support from governments, and discrimination is widespread. A disproportionate number of Roma are in prison, and this fuels the stereotype that they have a propensity towards criminality; in fact they are often the scapegoats for crime, and are frequently sentenced harshly. Roma have limited access to many public facilities, and have far

Romani community in Moldova nad Bodvou, Slovakia.

lower literacy levels than non-Roma: their culture places greater emphasis on the family unit than on formal education, so many young Roma do not attend school. This situation is even more pronounced in Eastern Europe, where those who seek education are often denied it. One recent issue is the Slovakian practice of placing Romani children in schools for the disabled, where the curricula give them fewer opportunities for educational development.[15]

In Hungary, the Czech Republic and Slovakia there has been an increase in reports of right-wing groups targeting the Roma in violent attacks that continue with little to impede them.[16] There is also persecution in Western Europe, often from the authorities. In Italy in 2008, for example, the government began to fingerprint Romani people, including children, as part of a census, in an initiative said to be an attempt to reduce crime. Evidently, stereotypes that characterize them as responsible for crime persist.[17]

There have also been numerous attacks on the camps where Roma live, often in poor conditions on the outskirts of cities. More recently, the French government began to demolish camps that are considered to be illegal settlements, and many Romani people have been repatriated to Romania and Bulgaria.[18] Repatriations have also occurred from Ireland, where persecution of Roma and Travellers remains widespread.[19] In the UK, the country's largest Roma and Traveller site, Dale Farm, was declared illegal in 2010 and subsequently cleared, despite high-profile protests.[20] Meanwhile, anti-Roma sentiment remains highly visible, in both public policy and the media.[21] On the same day that the British media reported the planned eviction of Roma living at Dale Farm, the *Daily Express* ran a front-page article with the headline 'Gypsy in £3m Benefit Fiddle'.[22]

Despite the prevalence of discrimination and persecution there are also increasing instances of Romani activism, and the Roma rights movement that has emerged in the past few decades seeks to raise awareness of the culture and issues surrounding the Roma. Romani organizations have been formed both globally and specifically in Eastern Europe, and the number of these continues to grow.[23] While the development of such groups has been slow, they remain in their infancy, and the recent increase in Romani activism suggests that understanding of the Roma can only be expected to develop. The World Romani Congress has met eight times since 1971, and has sought to promote the rights of Roma and their culture; the International Romani Union was founded at the second congress, in 1978. Meanwhile, the European Roma rights Centre aims to combat racism and human rights abuse against the Roma and supports activism. The Decade of Roma Inclusion, an initiative launched by European governments in 2005, was established with the aim of improving the status of Roma. It emphasized the importance of Roma participation to its success, and strove to engage with Romani organizations.

Following the decade's end in 2015, it was concluded that, although awareness of the situation of European Roma was raised, its ultimate objectives were not achieved.[24]

Although some obstacles have been overcome, there remains much work to be done in the field of Roma rights. One problem is that stereotyping remains rife, even in academic texts. For example, when discussing the progress that has been made in 1995, Derek Hawes and Barbara Perez wrote:

> The very notion of Gypsydom is antipathetic to the creation of a coherent programme of action or campaign for recognition and respect for Gypsies in the modern world. There is no Zionist dream to act as the central unifying nexus like that which sustained the Jews throughout a 2,000 year diaspora. No religious faith or body of literature unites, through time and space, a Romany people; even the common language is a poor fragmented thing, long since degenerated to a crude patois, only of philological interest.[25]

This passage sums up the difficulties that may be encountered in attempts to engage with the Roma as a single group – and this is the case with different styles of gypsy music too – but it also reveals the extent to which they are thought of as being disconnected and thoroughly separate, not only from non-Roma but also from each other. It is something of an ambiguous comment; Hawes and Perez seem to have an interest in Roma rights, but fall into the stereotypical discourse identified by Alaina Lemon, in which the Roma are detached from places and histories.[26] This reveals that even when intentions towards the Roma are good, the prevalence of stereotypes means that they are difficult to avoid. These stereotypes have come together to generate the imagined figure of the gypsy, which informs common attitudes towards the Roma.

There is therefore a significant disparity between the way
the Roma are perceived – as colourful, musical, romantic gypsies
who wander free of the constraints of society – and the situation
in which most contemporary Roma actually live. Roma do of
course continue to play music, but not because it is an inherent
part of their character or history; rather because it is a means of
making a living. Accordingly, the performance of gypsy music in
the Balkans has shifted to meet the expectation of contemporary
consumers and audiences: styles influenced by electronic music
and hip-hop, such as *manele* in Romania and *chalga* in Bulgaria,
are increasingly dominant. For Western audiences, however,
connections to history and tradition remain important.

Recent gypsy music performances touring in the West, and
programmed by Western non-Romani promoters, have sought
to move away from one-dimensional stereotypes by showcasing
diverse styles of gypsy music. The 'Gypsy Caravan' tour, put on
by the World Music Institute in 1999 and then reprised in 2002
with a different line-up, is a case in point. The 2002 tour, which
was documented in Jasmine Dellal's film *Gypsy Caravan: When
the Road Bends* (2006), featured five acts. Brass band Fanfare
Ciocărlia and *lăutari* (the Romanian word for a professional class
of Romani musicians whose music is played primarily on stringed
instruments) Taraf de Haïdouks are two of the most popular
gypsy music bands from Romania, but have quite different styles.
Flamenco was represented in the 'Gypsy Caravan' tour by Antonio
El Pipa and his band. The tour also involved Macedonian Romani
singer Esma Redžepova, who is so iconic a performer that she
became known as 'Queen of the Gypsies'.

However, the act least recognizable as a gypsy music group
was Maharaja, a band from Rajasthan. The tour deliberately
echoed the known migratory pattern of the Roma by featuring
Maharaja, whose music and performance is not in a style usually

associated with gypsy music. Their involvement seemed intended to show that threads can be found between the contemporary gypsy music of the Balkans and the music being played in the ancestral homeland of the Roma. It is almost impossible to say whether there is any truth in this thread. The Roma have been connected with music almost since their first arrival in Europe, but the question of whether they have their own particular music or whether they have adopted and adapted the styles of other peoples has been an ongoing question.

Whichever is the case, the associations between the Romani people and music, and between gypsy music and the Balkans, are undeniable. Music is almost synonymous with the gypsy figure, and it is true that musicianship is widespread among the Roma. Along with trades like ironmongery and horse-trading, music suited their nomadic lifestyle in the years before they became settled: it was an occupation that could be engaged in almost anywhere, and a skill for which demand was widespread. When large numbers of Roma were enslaved in the Ottoman Empire, many of them were made to play music for their owners, and those who were able to do so were particularly valued.[27] However, in the way the Roma are commonly presented, more importance is placed on the figure of the gypsy musician than on the nature of the music that they play.

There is documented evidence of music being a Romani occupation as far back as the fifteenth century, and tax registers of the Ottoman Empire recorded the occupations of Balkan Roma most often as musicians.'[28] Carol Silverman writes: 'We should not forget, however, that music has been a viable occupation for professional Roma for more than 600 years, and that in the current period of postsocialist transnational mobility it remains viable.'[29] There is possible evidence of Romani musicians as far back as 438 CE, in Persian histories describing musicians from India being transported to Persia for the entertainment of the king Bahram Gur. Their descendants became known as the Zott, while in one source they are referred to as the Luri, and *Zotti* and *Luri* remain Persian words equivalent to the English word 'gypsy'.[30] These connections are tenuous – and indeed this theory may well be wrong – but this is if nothing else further historic evidence of a deep-seated association between the Roma and musicianship: to describe the Roma as *Zotti* or *Luri* is to mark them out as musicians.[31]

There is firmer evidence of Roma in Constantinople in 1283, and it seems clear that from the fourteenth century onwards there were Romani people playing music in the Balkans. Silverman notes that 'From the fourteenth to the nineteenth centuries, Romanian Rom musician-slaves brought high prices.'[32] This is of course a very broad time span, but the context in which music was played by the Roma appears to have remained largely the same throughout this time, with Romani musicians playing for non-Romani audiences at events such as weddings and circumcisions. The manner in which gypsy music was played did not change until the abolition of slavery in the mid-nineteenth century, at which point Romani musicians began to be hired by peasants, and by the early 1900s string bands started to appear, replacing wind instruments.[33]

The manner in which the Roma played music might have been largely standardized across the Balkans, but the music they played was, and is, very varied. This was to some extent a consequence of the nomadic lifestyles that were historically more prevalent among Roma, and which exposed them to the range of musical styles that informed their repertoires.[34] But even those Roma who were settled or enslaved played a range of music. The instruments used, for example, varied from place to place, with string bands being dominant in Romania while in Macedonia the primary instruments of gypsy music were the *zurla*, a woodwind instrument, and the *tapan*, a kind of drum. There is evidence to suggest that both of these instruments were introduced to

Europe by the Roma, and the cimbalom and even the guitar might have first been played in Europe by Romani musicians. Whether or not this is the case, it is clear that the instrumental diversity of gypsy music is by no means a new phenomenon.

However, this does not mean that all current forms of gypsy music are part of a tradition that is centuries old. In many cases, styles that are firmly associated with gypsy music were not in fact played by the Roma until relatively recently. The Turkish influence that remains important in gypsy music was not absorbed into the music of the Roma until the eighteenth century, while the Serbian brass band tradition – which is itself derived from Ottoman influences – was not established until the 1940s.[35] Brass band music is today one of the best-known and most popular forms of gypsy music; it is played by Romani musicians in the Balkans and elsewhere, and the style has been adopted by non-Romani bands in the West, such as the Trans-Siberian March Band in London, and Slavic Soul Party in New York, whose names are evidently chosen to evoke a sense of the exotic. In the Balkans, the largest manifestation of brass band music is the Guča Trumpet Festival,

Zurla and *tapan*, played here at a Muslim circumcision ceremony in Kosovo.

an annual event in which a Serbian village of little more than two thousand inhabitants is taken over by brass musicians – many of them Romani – and thousands of spectators.

The Guča festival takes the form of a battle of the bands: brass bands compete in eliminating heats before a small number go forward to play at the festival. A jury then makes awards in numerous categories, of which the most prestigious are those for the best trumpet player, and for the best band, or *orkestar*. The best known of the Serbian brass bands is the Boban Marković Orkestar, more recently rebranded the Boban i Marko Marković Orkestar to take account of the increasing contributions of its founder's son. The Boban Marković Orkestar found fame at Guča, but has not competed since 2001, having won more awards then any other band, and now tours internationally.

Guča is seen as a place for brass bands to secure their reputations and for audiences to hear up-and-coming *orkestri*. The music is often played at a very fast tempo, and the build in pace that usually appears at several points in a brass band performance has become something of a signature of the style, but slower songs are also a part of most performances. The membership of the bands will typically range from around eight to fifteen performers and the instruments will typically include trumpets or flugelhorns, tenor horns, euphoniums, tubas or helicons and percussion. Occasionally they will also include saxophones, and vocals are sometimes a feature, although the music is primarily instrumental. But at Guča, and for many audiences of gypsy brass bands, it is the trumpets, and the musicians who play them, that are the stars.

Guča is by no means representative of how gypsy music is played in the Balkans; indeed, it was devised as a means of maintaining a single aspect of gypsy music. As Garth Cartwright explains, it was created to preserve the tradition of the *orkestar*: 'Tito's Yugoslavia was big on all things folkloric and some sharp-eared apparatchik, noting how the steady flow of humanity from rural to urban locations was depleting brass bands, came up with the idea of the festival/competition.'[36]

This distinction between rural and urban is interesting when considered in the context of work undertaken in Romania in the 1960s by folk revivalist A. L. Lloyd, who contrasts the urban *lăutari* who make their living playing in restaurants with the rural musicians who perform at weddings and dances. He claims that the rural *lăutari* have a stronger sense of tradition, while the urban musicians 'will play almost anything'.[37] Lloyd also examines the economics of rural *lăutari* in Romania; he found that music was a widespread trade amongst Roma, to the point that the profession was oversaturated. Playing music at weddings was lucrative but seasonal, so Romani musicians were not wealthy. Writing in 1964, he observes that, for many *lăutari*, moving to the city to make a living from music made good economic sense. 'To be a member of the State Folk Orchestra, the celebrated Barbu Lautaru band, is the golden dream of hundreds of gypsy minstrels,' he writes.[38] This contrasts sharply with the popular association between the gypsy and the idea of freedom: whereas the stereotypical gypsy musician is cast as an independent figure plying their trade on their own terms, an orchestra managed by a communist state (we will see another example of this when we discuss gypsy music in Russia) might in reality be a preferable mode of playing for Romani musicians.

When considering the apparent dichotomy between rural and urban in gypsy music, Carol Silverman's ethnographic fieldwork in Macedonia is of interest in that it straddles the two zones. Silverman conducted her work in Šuto Orizari, a municipality of Skopje, the capital of Macedonia. Locally known as Shutka, the area was first settled by Roma in the 1960s, following the Skopje earthquake of 1963, when displaced Roma were offered cheap housing there. It now has a majority Romani population, a strong Romani culture and a Romani mayor. In the early 1990s, Silverman found 'two types of Rom instrumental groups in Shutka, the *zurla* (double-reed conical-bore instrument, also known as *surla*) and *tapan* (double-headed cylindrical drum) trio, and the modern band'.[39] In these two kinds of ensemble – the traditional band playing instruments believed to date back at least as far as the arrival of the Roma in Europe, and the electrified group in which synthesizers take the place of certain instruments – we find a manifestation of the split between rural and urban, and between tradition and modernity.

There is also a physical manifestation of this split in Šuto Orizari. Located on the northern edge of Skopje, its location is effectively suburban, in between the city and the countryside. More-over, the poverty that dominates in the neighbourhood means that Šuto Orizari does not have the feeling of development typically

Šuto Orizari, Macedonia.

associated with a European city, despite being a built-up area. This sense of being neither urban nor rural, neither one thing nor the other, exemplifies the externalized, Othered situation of the Roma.

Mattijs van de Port has conducted primarily urban fieldwork in Serbia, and explores the relationship between Romani musicians and the non-Roma who form their audience. This turns out to be complex and contradictory: the Roma are regarded as Others, but it is in their Otherness that their musical talent is identified and celebrated. Van de Port contrasts the usual attitude towards the Roma displayed by non-Roma in Serbia – whereby the gypsy is seen as dirty and criminal, and interaction with Roma is seen as taboo – with the way in which they respond to Romani musicians playing gypsy music, declaring their love for the Roma and even displaying physical affection.[40] This is interesting not only in the apparent paradox that it exemplifies, but in that it reveals that the gypsy musician remains an attractive, romantic figure to those within the Balkans as well as to those outside the region.

For van de Port, this romanticized Otherness that is seen in gypsy music can also be found in popular music more widely:

> The suggestion that a relationship exicsts [sic] between Otherness and the attribution of musical talent is further endorsed by the fact that musicians who cannot be readily distinguished as 'other' often mark their being-different by way of special clothing and deviant behaviour.[41]

He goes on to suggest that 'society *recruits* musicians *from* the margins.'[42] This suggestion fits neatly with the history we have seen in which Roma played music as slaves: indeed, slaves are also recruited from the margins of society. In the case of the Roma, the marginalized status from which they were recruited as slaves is reinforced further by the ongoing association between the gypsy and music.

The studies undertaken by Lloyd, Silverman and van de Port cover three Balkan countries and span a forty-year period in the latter half of the twentieth century. We might therefore expect to find differences in how professional Romani musicians perform music and how it is received; indeed there are some differences in the instrumentation used and in the environments in which gypsy music operates, which vary depending on whether they are urban or rural. However, there is a correlation between all three: in each case the Roma seem to present a sense of tradition. For Lloyd, the rural *lăutari* maintain what is regarded as tradition even as the gypsy music economy evolves for their urban counterparts; Silverman finds that this sense of tradition persists in the semi-urban environment of Shutka, in the continuing use of the *zurla* and *tapan*, and in van de Port's work, urban gypsy musicians seem to provide a longed-for sense of the traditional for the non-Romani audiences who typically regard the Roma with disdain outside the context of musical performance.

The desire expressed by some Roma to move away from the rural environment and improve their economic prospects in the city can be seen as a further step in their migratory pattern. We should not forget that migration does not necessarily entail a crossing of borders, and this fact should hold even truer for the Roma, a people who are not directly affiliated with a unified nation state. Of course, such migratory patterns are by no means confined to the Romani people: the movement of Balkan Roma from rural to urban locations is part of a far wider global trend: the shift from life in rural, agrarian communities, to a different kind of economy in the space of the city. However, this kind of movement by Roma might be seen as surprising: having been regarded as Others for so long they are not perceived as fitting comfortably into the contemporary city. This is part of an expectation that the gypsy should be seen to uphold a more traditional lifestyle.

Garth Cartwright's account of Guča is interesting in this context. He writes of the rural landscape in which Guča sits:

Nostalgia for Titoism is, I imagine, strong here, the greying population containing those who recall the brutality of fascism and the way Tito brought order, built roads and schools, ensured none went hungry. Milošević's era was turbo-folk, turbo-war, turbo-inflation. Bullshit bullshit bullshit.[43]

Cartwright goes on to describe how stalls at the festival sell T-shirts and key rings bearing the faces of Radovan Karadžić and Ratko Mladić, presumably aimed at tourists from outside the region.[44] He is explicit in not condoning this trade in nostalgia for the conflict of the 1990s, and this contrasts with his implicit approval of Tito, in which 'the brutality of fascism' is muted by the development that Tito spearheaded. His caveat, 'I imagine', is also telling: he does not write of this nostalgia with any certainty, but simply perceives it in the rural Balkan landscape. This is an expectation of attachments to the past, which ties in with expectations of tradition. However, the kitsch nostalgia for Karadžić and Mladić indicates that such expectations do evolve – even if they remain inaccurate.

The Roma and the Balkans have in common the fact that both are commonly cast in a certain way; they have identities imposed on them from outside. But there is of course a practice of identity creation among the Roma, who construct their own identities as musicians. This has been observed among *lăutari* in Romania, who are clearly conscious of the perceived connection to tradition that they inhabit with their music.[45]

The word *lăutari* is used in Romania to refer to all professional Romani musicians, including those who play contemporary, hip-hop influenced music; but in the way the word is marketed to Western audiences, tradition is important. This kind of *lăutari* music sometimes features woodwind and accordions, but it is principally played on stringed instruments. Most integral to the *lăutari* sound are violins and the cimbalom, an instrument whose strings are stretched across a box – rather like a grand piano with its lid lifted – and struck with hammers in a similar fashion to a xylophone. The cimbalom's sound is bouncing, pizzicato and percussive, and when it is played at a fast tempo – as is often the case in gypsy music – it produces an almost buzzing sound that contributes to the frenetic mood that the music sometimes evokes.

Unlike the Balkan brass bands, which have a clear origin in Ottoman martial music, *lăutari* music is rooted in a less well-defined gypsy music tradition. It is perhaps for this reason that it has been so connected to a sense of tradition: the fact that its history is nebulous means that its origin is more prone to being mythologized, and the idea of tradition becomes more important than the actual history of the music. Indeed, the notion of tradition is so valued in *lăutari* music, and gypsy music more broadly, because it is something that can be clung to in the absence of a verified history that can be learned and understood.

The sound and instrumentation of *lăutari* string band music reinforces this notion. Whereas the brass band music showcased at Guča is mechanical in its instruments and connected to the organized military in its origins, the wood and gut of the stringed instruments of the *lăutari* may be perceived as closer to nature, and the violins and cimbaloms as more primitive instruments, not too far removed from the similar instruments that were fashioned centuries ago. There is thus something artisanal about the *lăutar*; great skill and an indistinct yet important tradition combine to bring about a sense of the authentic.

Contemporary *lăutari* are certainly aware of this, but as professional musicians and performers their focus is to a large extent on gaining work and generating an income, hence their adaptability and willingness to abandon tradition in favour of more fashionable sounds. In order to raise their status and value, they seek out social privilege by asserting their self-perceived position as an elite within the Romani community. From outside, however, their musical skills are romanticized by non-Roma, but as individuals the *lăutari* are regarded with the same disdain as those Roma who do not play music. Ironically, some *lăutari* share these views about other Roma. While Romani musicians might suffer from outside perceptions, we should remember that they do have some stake in their own identities.

This dichotomy of identity imposition from outside and identity creation from within becomes even more complex when taken in the context of Romani music from the Balkans being a product that is exported to the West. Julia Heuwekemeijer has considered the case of the contemporary Romanian group Taraf de Haïdouks, who play on stringed instruments in the *lăutari* tradition.

The musicians in Taraf de Haïdouks are motivated on one level by their need to earn money and maintain their audiences, but a side effect of their performances in the West is that it proves to other Roma in Romania that their music has a substantial Western audience – in contrast to its position in Romania, where acoustic, classically styled gypsy music has been surpassed in popularity by more electronic styles. This ensures that the idea of a *lăutari* tradition is propagated; the fact of the Western audience keen to pay to hear Romani string bands means that it is more appealing for further generations of Roma to continue playing it. The sense of the tradition continuing for deep-seated cultural reasons integral to Romani identity might be an illusion for the benefit of Western audiences, but the tradition of Roma playing music endures as a result of the way it is played.[46]

Moreover, the group has been able to profit from Western expectations of tradition. One element of their performance involves a violinist encouraging members of the audience to stick banknotes on his bow, presenting it as if this is an established part of the gypsy music performance. On one hand this reflects an actual means of engagement between performers of gypsy music and their audiences in the Balkans: at weddings and concerts in the region, musicians are handed cash by guests, and at the Guča festival brass bands are similarly rewarded with banknotes by revellers. On the other hand, the encouragement of this manner of engagement by Taraf de Haïdouks means that the tradition is extended because the audience has been persuaded to engage with it, and it is the possibility of engagement with tradition that attracts audiences to do so.[47] The musician, Heuwekemeijer says, is 'actively participating within constructions of authenticity'.[48]

The notion of the authentic has specific implications when applied to music. Simon Frith has written: 'The rock aesthetic depends, crucially, on an argument about authenticity. Good music is the authentic expression of something – a person, an idea, a feeling, a shared experience, a *Zeitgeist*. Bad music is inauthentic – it expresses nothing.'[49] In this argument the opposition between authentic and inauthentic is expressed in terms of a straightforward dichotomy of good and bad. In gypsy music, and more broadly in world music, there are many examples where the idea of authenticity becomes blurred. Western record labels purport to sell consumers authentic products that represent the experiences of another culture, and on one level these products are indeed authentic representations of Romani music, played by Romani musicians who are singing of their own experiences. However, this authenticity is filtered through the gaze of the record label, and there are arguments that this makes the music less authentic.

Clearly the direct contrast between good and bad music is not applicable here. It is difficult to argue that a piece of gypsy music played live by musicians in the setting of their own community is better than, or superior to, the same piece of music played by the same musicians on a recording. Indeed, the argument that one is more authentic than the other is tenuous, but because the figure of the gypsy is seen as a conduit to tradition, freedom and authentic experiences, authenticity becomes a more loaded term when applied to gypsy music.

Tradition and authenticity, as individual concepts, are evidently both important to the reception of gypsy music by non-Roma, particularly those in the West. Additionally, the connection between the Roma and the Balkans begins to be illuminated when we consider Cartwright's description of Guča. The sense of tradition invoked at a gypsy music festival reveals outside perceptions not only about the Roma but also about the Balkans, and it is apparent that the two are perceived in similar ways. Among the common perceptions that surround the Roma is that they are seen as a people who are more deeply connected to tradition than non-Roma, and there is an expectation that this will be conveyed in their music. This is of course a further example of the romanticization and Othering of the Roma: they are seen as a source of tradition and authenticity, and they act as a route by which Western audiences can reach apparent traditions within the contemporary world music economy.

As we have already seen, romanticization of this kind is by no means a recent perception, and nor is the connection between the Roma and tradition. This will become clearer as we step a little way outside of the Balkans and into Hungary. Such a detour is necessary in order to approach more clearly the question of what gypsy music is. Moreover, it will reveal that this is a question that has been debated by non-Roma for many years, and that it is bound up with questions of tradition and authenticity.

2 LISZT VS BARTÓK: THE HUNGARIAN QUESTION

We now step outside of the Balkans, and into Hungary, the country on which studies into what constitutes gypsy music have tended to centre. The likely reasons for this are the significant Romani population in Hungary and the fact that the music played by many Hungarian Roma has been enduringly popular outside of Romani communities. However, as is the case with other countries where gypsy music is played, different styles can be heard.

The lexicon of Hungarian folk and gypsy musics adds confusion to the numerousness of styles. The differences between Romungre and Vlach music are simple to observe and articulate: Romungre is polished, orchestrated and generally played by string bands, whereas Vlach music is traditionally restricted to rhythmic vocals and percussion, often using improvised instruments such as spoons. But in Hungarian music, terms like *verbunkos*, *nóta* and *style hongrois* are used alongside Romungre, and the distinctions between these terms are easier to blur.

Romungre refers not only to a style of music but also to one of the groups of Roma settled in Hungary; while Romungre music has its origins in this group it may of course be played by non-Romungre musicians. Romungre music is perhaps the archetypal gypsy music, if not the most authentic – if there can even be such a thing as an authentic gypsy music. It can loosely be equated with the string band music that has been recognizable

Musicians from the Budapest Gypsy Symphony Orchestra, 2012.

as gypsy music across Europe for at least two hundred years; Hungarian gypsy music spread across Europe from the late eighteenth century onwards (contemporaneously with Russian gypsy choir music and flamenco, two genres which will be examined further through this book).[1]

Romungre music is tied to the term *verbunkos*, which has been used since the early twentieth century to describe music played in the Hungarian gypsy music tradition. The name derives from the German word *Werbung*, meaning 'recruitment', as the music was played during military recruiting expeditions, often, although not exclusively, by Romani musicians.[2] It is a dance style, and its lively sound was intended to be appealing to potential recruits. Although it was often played by Romani musicians, it is less directly a Romani style, with many examples being written by non-Romani composers such as János Bihari and Béla Bartók.

Another term relevant to discussion of Hungarian gypsy music is *nóta*, which describes the repertoire played and claimed by Romani musicians in Hungary.[3] The sound and style of *nóta* can be varied, since, like gypsy music more broadly, it is defined in terms of the musicians playing it, rather than in terms of its musical characteristics. The difference, however, is that while what constitutes gypsy music is generally defined by non-Roma, the parameters of *nóta* are set and understood by Romani musicians.

Often used interchangeably with Romungre music, the term *style hongrois*, or Hungarian style, is more specifically used to refer to music by non-Romani composers like Liszt and Brahms, whose work is influenced by Hungarian folk music and which is understood to have connotations of gypsiness.[4] It is a style that popularized elements of Romungre, *verbunkos* and *nóta* music in the eighteenth and nineteenth centuries. While more of a classical music than a gypsy music, and one which is also informed by music from outside Hungary, *style hongrois* demarcates a porous borderline between the two.

Romungre-style music continues to be played in Hungary and elsewhere by both Romani and non-Romani musicians. Although primarily string-led, played on violins and cimbaloms, it also includes woodwind and vocals. Its popularity is not difficult to comprehend: lilting and melodic, with strong rhythmic elements, and with reference points in both classical and folk music, it is an accessible form of music yet one with complex elements in its rich instrumentation and its entwined melodies and counter-melodies. Another feature that has ensured its enduring appeal is the sense of the exotic with which it is imbued for many listeners.

Playing the cimbalom
in Hungary.

Ironically, any sense of the exotic is often absent from
contemporary performances of gypsy music in Hungary. Many
restaurants in Budapest promise that gypsy music will be played
to accompany diners' meals, but this music frequently derives
from the classical tradition and its relationship with gypsy music.
Sometimes it deviates further, with Strauss waltzes, for example,
being part of the repertoire along with Liszt and Brahms. While
the Romungre style has not died and can still be heard being
played by some musicians, the notion of gypsy music in this
context – in which the audience consists largely of tourists – is

broadened in the extreme. It is almost as though any classical music that has been billed as gypsy music and which is performed by musicians who might ostensibly be Roma is accepted as gypsy music by its intended audience, and an Eastern or Central European location is enough to suggest the exotic and in turn gypsy music to Western audiences.

But these audiences are attracted to gypsy music based on a set of characteristics that was codified decades ago, and which have in fact been adopted by classical composers. The characteristics of this gypsy music style were succinctly outlined by Franz Liszt, who wrote of 'the three principal points which constitute the Bohemian character'. According to Liszt these are: 'Intervals – not used in European harmony'; 'Rhythm – proper to the race'; and 'Ornamentation – luxuriant and eminently Oriental'.[5] Significantly, Liszt describes the music not in terms of what it is, but in terms of what it is not (this recalls Fraser and Hancock's attempts at defining the identity of the Romani people). It is Oriental rather than European, and suited to the gypsy race. Yet the description is in some ways broadly correct.

The intervals that Liszt describes are indeed different to those commonly found in classical music, and can be found in what has become known as the gypsy scale, which musicologist Shay Loya describes as 'typified by the symmetrical placement of two augmented seconds'.[6] Equally, the rhythms used within the *verbunkos* tradition, and also in other forms of gypsy music, differ from classical norms. However, the notion of the gypsy scale has recently been seen as redundant and unhelpful. Loya notes that 'crucially, the name itself also predetermines the reading, because – amazingly enough – there is no nonethnic generic term for this scale.'[7] Meanwhile, Carol Silverman describes it as a 'misnomer', pointing out that many other scales are used by Romani musicians, and that the gypsy scale is not commonly used in the Balkans.[8] Silverman's survey of the music of Balkan Roma also includes a comprehensive list of rhythms used in the čoček genre, a style of music and dance found throughout the Balkans.[9]

The rhythms used in čoček, and indeed in other Balkan and Hungarian gypsy music, are varied, but some trends can be identified. Syncopation is very prevalent, with stresses placed on beats at irregular points in the rhythmic sequence, and in many cases the music is played in complex time signatures, which serve to bring out the syncopation even further. Tempos are variable, with some rhythms being used at both faster and slower speeds. These elements bring about the feeling that gypsy music is unpredictable and wild, a feeling that aligns with stereotypes about the Roma, but which also explains the popularity of the music.

These observations are merely snippets of the discourse around gypsy music. However, they serve to illustrate two points that should be borne in mind here: firstly, that the gypsy music of Hungary which is key to the debates we shall consider is not representative of all Balkan gypsy music or indeed of all Hungarian gypsy music; and secondly, that the numerous styles of music described as gypsy which can be found in any given region do not easily fit into a simple definition or set of characteristics such as those offered by Liszt. However, we will consider the case of Hungary here because the questions that it provokes regarding tradition, authenticity, nationhood, and the position of the Roma themselves, are relevant to wider concerns about gypsy music and to its links with the Balkans.

The two key figures in this debate are Liszt and subsequently Béla Bartók. Their contributions to the debate are not solely focused on the question of what Romani music is; as we shall see, their arguments take in their broader attitudes to the Roma, along with questions of Hungarian nationalism, and of their own places within the national and folk music of Hungary. However, at the heart of their hypotheses is the question of whether the

Roma have a music that can be described as their own. It was Liszt's view that the music regarded as Hungarian folk music had its origins with the Roma, whereas Bartók asserted that the Roma did not have a role in the creation of this music, but simply adopted and played the music of non-Roma.

In considering this question, I will seek to distinguish between forms of music specific to the Roma, which might be regarded as 'Romani music', and styles associated with but not necessarily originating with the Roma, which I term 'gypsy music'. These two terms are usually conflated and regarded as 'gypsy music': any music taken to have a gypsy sound – for example, the presence of augmented second intervals or a čoček rhythm – is generally regarded as such without reference to whether or not it is being played by Romani musicians. Similarly, when Romani people play music, it is in general thought of as gypsy music, whether or not it has the characteristics that might objectively be applied to that style. There is no single gypsy music style either within or beyond the Balkans, but by surveying the issues of ownership and appropriation that surround ownership of gypsy music, we may be able to bring clarity to the question of how we define it.

The characteristics identified by Liszt in gypsy music – or as he termed it, Bohemian music – were printed in his book *Des Bohémiens et de leur musique en Hongrie*, which was first published in 1859 and updated in 1881. Liszt uses the term *Bohémien* in the original French text, but although *Bohémiens* is translated as 'Gipsy' in the English title, *The Gipsy in Music*, the translator, Edwin Evans, uses 'Bohemian' throughout. While 'gypsy' is probably a more accurate translation in the context of gypsy music (Bohemian music is not a recognized genre or style of music), 'Bohemian' is derived from the French word and denotes non-conformity of the type we have seen in such gypsy figures as

Franz Liszt.

Augustus John and George Borrow. In this text Liszt declared that all Hungarian music was derived from the music of the Roma.

As if aware of the controversy that his book would provoke, Liszt writes: 'We do not disguise from ourselves that the theory of Hungarian national songs being purely of Bohemian origin is much more hazardous than that of the Zingani being the authors of their own dance music.'[10] However, he then goes on to declare his agreement with

> Those who hold that even the most modest national songs of Hungary – those therefore upon which modern art has not

the faintest claim – have been originally borrowed from the Bohemians; deliberately borrowed by those who fitted them to Hungarian words.[11]

Elsewhere in the book he elaborates, implying that it is not a tangible aspect of the music that marks out Hungarian folk music as having its foundation in gypsy music:

> Whoever may have been the first inventors of these melodies or the first creators of their scale . . . the Bohemians have none the less a right to claim this music as their own; since they alone have given it life, enabling it to move the soul and electrify the heart of man.[12]

Here, Liszt seems to acknowledge that in technical terms the music might not be intrinsically or originally gypsy. Yet he credits the Roma as the progenitors of Hungarian music based on the response that their playing elicits. This continues to be a recurring trope, with commentators commonly describing emotion, or a similar concept, as an integral part of gypsy music. Such claims are difficult to wholly dismiss, due to the unquantifiable nature that they apply to gypsy music, but they come across as vague and hardly authoritative.

Moreover, the notion that gypsy music is defined by emotion is tied up with persistent stereotypes about the Roma: to relate any style of music so strongly to emotion is to deny it any intellectual worth. Liszt's assertion that gypsy music can 'move the soul and electrify the heart' is not too far removed from the association between gypsies and magic; it is evoking spiritual rather than cerebral or logical responses to the music.

There are many more instances of stereotyping in Liszt's book; from the outset he is dismissive of all aspects of Romani culture other than gypsy music, and his descriptions fall into a noble savage discourse.[13] Even when he begins to describe the music, for which he clearly has genuine admiration, he remains dismissive. According to Liszt, instrumental gypsy music is not sophisticated enough to tell us anything about the Romani people – he credits its wide-ranging appeal as the flipside of this – and he is more disparaging still of the non-instrumental music, the songs and ballads, of the Roma: 'These rare specimens of songs, rudely forged in their own language, or borrowed from others, are, however, no more than rough sketches; quite undeserving to be ranked as works of art.'[14] He goes on to argue directly that the depth of emotion he finds in the music of the Roma is in direct opposition to intellect and civilization:

> It was quite natural that a people leading a debased and cruel existence should have chosen this art in preference to any other, when it desired for itself some means of ennobling those primitive instincts of its being which had remained so long buried in silent mystery.[15]

And subsequently: 'Music was the only art accessible to [the gypsy]; because music alone awakens emotion by sensation, without requiring the intervention of any idea.'[16]

There is certainly a personal agenda to Liszt's book; he is writing in response to his own position in relation to Hungary and the dominant musical culture of his time. *Des Bohémiens* was initially begun as an essay intended to accompany Liszt's *Hungarian Rhapsodies*, a suite of nineteen piano pieces influenced by the *verbunkos* style, first published between 1851 and 1853, and then between 1882 and 1886.[17]

As piano pieces, the *Rhapsodies* might not sound particularly like gypsy music to the casual listener approaching them as pieces written in the classical tradition by a classical composer. But even in Liszt's use of rhapsody form, which typically involves a range of moods, and which was still a relatively recent form in 1851, they have a connection to gypsy music; the contrasts between fast and slow, and between gentle and furious, which are recognized as features of gypsy music, can be observed in the *Rhapsodies*. Moreover, there are particular passages that more closely connect them to the gypsy music tradition. In 'Rhapsody No. 19', for instance, a slower motif that uses the gypsy scale is followed by a rapid passage in which the piano mimics the fast, tightly knitted manner in which the cimbalom is often played in the *verbunkos* style. 'Rhapsody No. 7', meanwhile, features glissandos that echo the urgent bowing of a violin, and all of the *Rhapsodies* have slower passages that seem more inspired by the vocal tradition in Romani music. Fourteen of the nineteen are in minor keys, so as to render the use of the gypsy scale more pronounced.

Liszt's book was, in a way, a defence of the *Rhapsodies*, an explanation for why they could be described as Hungarian despite bearing many of the hallmarks of gypsy music, a form of music that has always been seen as connected to Otherness. It was important for Liszt to assert his identity as a Hungarian: having been born in a German-speaking part of the Austro-Hungarian Empire and into a family that is likely to have had German ancestry, his native language was German and he never learned Hungarian. He had also spent many years away from Hungary, living a largely itinerant life as a touring pianist. Therefore, when Liszt describes gypsy music as Hungarian music, there is a subtext: Liszt's music – the music of a composer who seemed not entirely Hungarian in the same way the Roma of Hungary seemed not entirely Hungarian – is also presented as Hungarian music.

His relationship to music, playing and composition, is also implicit in his presentation of gypsy music. This is most apparent in his concern with the idea of the virtuoso. It is the virtuosity of gypsy musicians, Liszt claims, that gives gypsy music its particular character, bringing to it the key elements of rhythm and ornamentation:

> It was Bohemian virtuosi who festooned Bohemian melody with their florid ornaments seeming to throw upon each, as it were, the prism of a rainbow or the scintillation of a multi-coloured sash. It was Bohemian virtuosi who brought out the various rhythms, whether sharply-cut or softly cadenced; whether lightly detached or gracefully linked together; which give to their music its profile and its attitude. They alone have interpreted this art, as alone could artists who understand its language, including all its secret murmurings and asides.[18]

Additionally, he describes a collaborative aspect between composer and virtuoso, arguing that the ambitions of the former cannot be fulfilled without the involvement of the latter: 'In short, without the virtuoso the composer's existence would be a perpetual hell; his creative genius being unable by itself either to actuate what it conceived or to objectify that by which it is filled.'[19] This focus on the virtuoso is significant for two reasons. Firstly, Liszt found success as a virtuoso before he became established as a composer; he toured Europe as a concert pianist before writing his major works, including the *Hungarian Rhapsodies*.[20] Indeed, the *Rhapsodies* are complex compositions that require a good degree of skill or virtuosity from the pianist, for instance in the dense passages that mimic the sound of the cimbalom. Liszt's itinerant lifestyle, by which he made a living playing music and was applauded for his considerable skill, meant that he had something in common with the stereotypical gypsy musician during this period – although it is unlikely that any such comparisons were made at the time – and with this in mind it is easy to see why he gave so much more credit to Romani musicians than had previously been the case.

Secondly, he came to appreciate the traditional music of the *verbunkos* style through composed music in the first instance, and only later via Romani musicians.[21] Accordingly, his argument that Hungarian music has its origins with the Roma follows his own pattern of discovery, which begins with the composer acting as architect of Hungarian folk music and then reverts to placing the virtuoso in this role. It is arguable that in his defence of gypsy music, Liszt sought to validate the trajectory of his own creative development and output, first as a musician and then as a composer.[22] He also sought to justify his relationship to the Hungarian nation, as a Hungarian who (like the Roma of Hungary) had always seemed to be slightly outside of Hungarian nationality and identity. But it is indeed the case that Liszt's own work is given a sense of greater credence, and perhaps a greater authenticity, when it is considered as part of a tradition established by Romani virtuosi. If it can be said that there is a gypsy music canon then, rightly or wrongly, Liszt's *Hungarian Rhapsodies* would certainly be included within it – despite the fact that they were not composed by a Rom, and even though they are written in the tradition of the composer rather than that of the virtuoso.

Liszt's treatise on gypsy music provoked immediate controversy, and debate has continued to this day. Béla Bartók's contributions to this debate are the best known, and he serves as a figurehead in opposition to Liszt's viewpoint. Like Liszt, he has become associated with gypsy music as a composer due to the influence of Hungarian folk music – music that Liszt argued was gypsy in its origin – on his compositions. However, Bartók insisted that the music widely regarded as gypsy music was in fact not intrinsic to the Romani people. In the early twentieth century Bartók and his colleague Zoltán Kodály made field recordings of Hungarian folk music, which they concluded to be distinct from the music of the

Roma. Reporting on his findings, Bartók begins an essay on gypsy music as follows:

> To start without preliminaries, I should like to state that what people (including Hungarians) call 'gipsy music' is not gipsy music but Hungarian music; it is not old folk music but a fairly recent type of Hungarian popular art music composed, practically without exception, by Hungarians of the upper middle class. But while a Hungarian gentleman may compose music, it is traditionally unbecoming to his social status to perform it 'for money' – only gipsies are supposed to do that.[23]

However, he goes on to acknowledge that

> there is real gipsy music too, songs on gipsy texts, but these are known to and sung by the non-musician rural gipsies only, the regular gipsy bands never play them in public. What they do play is the work of Hungarian composers, and consequently Hungarian music.[24]

So Bartók does not refute the notion of an actual authentic gypsy music; only the idea that the *verbunkos*-style music that was often played by Romani musicians originates with the Roma themselves.

As we saw to be the case with Liszt, there are issues of Hungarian nationalism at stake in Bartók's views, which are bound up in the relationship between his compositions and the idea of gypsy music. Bartók's initial motivation for re-establishing Hungarian music as distinct from gypsy music can be seen as nationalist: by refiguring the style described as 'gypsy' as a national music, he situates Hungary and 'true' Hungarians as the progenitors of this style. The role of imitator was ascribed to Romani artists and, by association, to Liszt, with their inconsistently and insufficiently Hungarian identities.[25] But the eventual aims of Bartók's ethnographic fieldwork and field recordings of Hungarian folk songs went beyond refuting Liszt; in seeking to demonstrate the Hungarian folk origins of gypsy music, he came to aspire to the development of this style into an original, yet truly Hungarian, form of music.[26] Bartók's work was not necessarily driven by the reclamation of Hungarian music, but rather by a desire to create a Hungarian music of his own.

Somewhat paradoxically, this chimes with Liszt's desire to identify a Hungarian music; the difference is that whereas Liszt ascribed the creation of such a music to the Roma, Bartók undertook the more ambitious task of creating it himself. Accordingly, Liszt's compositions, inspired as they were by the

Bela Bartók.

music he identified as gypsy music, might be more likely to
fit within the gypsy music envelope than Bartók's consciously
evolved work.

Like Liszt, Bartók composed in the rhapsody form, most
notably with his 1904 'Rhapsody, Op. 1', for piano, which used
elaborate sequences and scales just as Liszt's *Rhapsodies* did.
But Bartók used his folk music field recordings as the basis for
some of his later works, which were in fact arrangements of
the folk songs and dances he had heard rural musicians play.
These included songs and dances from Romania, Slovakia and
Ukraine, as well as Hungarian pieces, but it is the latter that are
most significant in the context of Bartók's ambition to create a
national music for Hungary. Many of his arrangements of folk
songs are presented specifically as Hungarian, and are devoid of
gypsy music character, but this is not necessarily the case with his
source materials.

Indeed, many of the field recordings might have lent themselves equally well to being transposed to the *verbunkos* style, and
Bartók's decision to foreground a Hungarian character in his
arrangements is clearly very deliberate. It is difficult to speculate
on whether there are Romani or gypsy music antecedents to any
of the pieces that Bartók recorded, but the likelihood is that in
some cases there are, since Romani musicians would no doubt
have been present in the regions in which he made his recordings,
and these musicians might have carried music from place to place,
making it their own in the process. But Bartók's stance on gypsy
music in fact extended beyond the question of origin and as far
as the style of playing:

> There remains the possibility of a designation like 'Gypsy
> performance'. Yet there is a catch here, too. The mode of
> performance customarily designated the 'Gypsy way' will
> be encountered in its purest form in city Gypsy bands.

The further we move from the urban cultural centers, the
simpler this 'way' becomes until, finally, we find a Gypsy
performance in remote villages that is in no way different
from peasant performance. Thus, it seems that even the mode
of performance depends not on race but seemingly on the
environment. This leads to the conclusion that even the so-
called Gypsy-style performance is of Hungarian origin and is
the mode of performance of the Hungarian gentry class.[27]

This passage is significant in what it tells us about gypsy music
for two reasons. Firstly, it goes against the common perception
that gypsy music can be defined with reference to the emotional
response it provokes. Even the distinct style of playing that is
widely thought to epitomize gypsy music is perhaps a creation
of non-Romani musicians. Secondly, it draws us back to the
dichotomy of rural and urban that we have already discussed.
Once again, the rural performance is seen as more authentic,
without the ornamentation and commercialization of the urban
gypsy music. However, Bartók sees this more authentic music
as a non-Romani music. This is a quite striking contrast with the
popular viewpoint that equates gypsies and tradition. Bartók's
standpoint is generally more widely accepted than Liszt's, despite
the fact that it dissociates the gypsy figure from the enduring
trope in which the gypsy is a carrier of tradition in music.

Bartók not only presented the Roma as lacking in a musical
culture of their own; he also suggested that they had a negative
influence on Hungarian music. It was already understood that
gypsy musicians appropriated diverse musical styles as required by
their profession, but Bartók now suggested that this appropriation
had the effect of contaminating musical styles with the sham
veneer of gypsiness.[28] Liszt's crediting of Hungarian music to
Romani virtuosi did nothing to bolster the way that their music
was received; on the contrary, his argument actually left Romani

musicians open to further criticism – even though their music was not necessarily of their own foundation.

From the Romani standpoint, there is no argument in which they receive a truly equitable critical treatment. Liszt's dismissal of a Hungarian folk tradition, and idealization of gypsy music in its place, provoked a backlash in which gypsies were blamed for their corruption of that very tradition. This is a sign that the popular association between Romani people and musical talent is perhaps not the positive counterpart to more negative stereotypes that it might sometimes appear to be. Even the musicianship of the Roma can be turned against them in more than one way.

Nevertheless, in Bartók's work there are indications that the place of the Roma in the hierarchy of others can be open to change. Brown describes how he adapted his views in response to the arrival in Europe of American popular music: 'With a new ethnic other to fear, Bartók found himself able to celebrate Gypsy music for being at least in some way Hungarian.'[29] This is comparable with the distinction made by Liszt between gypsies and Jews, with the latter being described as mere imitators while the former were deemed capable of original creation. Despite the different viewpoints propounded by the two Hungarian composers, they have in common their deployment of gypsy music as a means of asserting their Hungarian identities and nullifying the music and identities of other groups.

'For Roma-rights advocates, the investigation that starts from the question "What is Gypsy music" may be already biased and biasing, it judges without knowing its prejudgement.'[30] This is a point made by David Malvinni early on in his book *The Gypsy Caravan*. Perhaps the Roma-rights advocates who have contributed so much to change in other areas deem music to be less consequential; at any rate, it is interesting that while 'Roma' is generally considered to be a preferable designation to 'gypsy', it apparently remains perfectly acceptable for both record labels and consumers to talk of 'gypsy music' rather than 'Romani music'. This suggests that while the Roma are now being seen more accurately as having an intrinsic culture, the music they play remains something that is constructed and commodified from outside.

We might hypothesize a distinction between Romani music, which would refer to any music played by Romani people, and gypsy music, which would refer to the music associated with the gypsy figure. However, this hypothesis does not withstand development beyond this basic distinction. It is of course perfectly possible for Romani musicians to play music of any genre: for example, classical, jazz or soul. Indeed, it is possible to identify commonalities between these genres and the style referred to simply as gypsy music, and subsequently we will see that a single piece of music might be both Romani music and gypsy music. Contemporary *lăutari* Taraf de Haïdouks have engaged with classical music, brass band Fanfare Ciocărlia have incorporated and covered jazz, and the singing of Esma Redžepova is often described as soulful. So despite the difficulties in defining gypsy music, it is in fact a more helpful term than Romani music from a musicological point of view, in that it constitutes a genre in and of itself whilst being receptive to engagement with other genres. However, the ideas propounded by Liszt and Bartók testify to its enduring controversy as a concept.

Bartók's viewpoint was subsequently supported by A. L. Lloyd, who extended Bartók's arguments about gypsy music to the Balkans and elsewhere in Eastern Europe, stating:

> In general, the gypsies borrow from the music of whatever people they happen to be living among; thus, Bulgarian gypsies play a different music from their cousins in Russia, and the repertory of Albanian gypsies does not correspond to that of the gypsies of Slovakia. In Rumania, as elsewhere,

the gypsies have for centuries played whatever their customers wanted to hear. Like a true professional, the gypsy minstrel considers music as a commodity rather than as a heritage, and in consequence he is hardly likely to have preserved much of his own ethnic musical culture.[31]

This is an interesting point in that Lloyd adheres to the stereo-typical view that the Roma do not have a strong connection to their heritage. This is in line with Liszt's views on the Roma, and indeed Lloyd neglects Bartók's point that there is a 'real gypsy music' in addition to the different styles played by different groups of Roma in different countries. Despite his unenlightened insinuations about Romani identity, this is perhaps a more plausible argument. But even if there is no truly authentic gypsy music, and thus no clear-cut and genuine Romani music, it is clear that there are many kinds of gypsy music – the various forms that have developed in countries where Roma have worked as performing artists and which have continued to be performed by and associated with the gypsy.

If there is, or ever was, also a music native to the Roma themselves, then this is much harder to identify. If there was ever such a music then it has certainly become hybridized with the other forms that have been adopted by Romani musicians, just as those forms may have been influenced by the music of the Roma, the hypothetical Romani music. The Roma have long been thought of as magpie-like, gathering and hoarding musical styles, and this characteristic complements their perception in the popular imagination as nomads and thieves. But it is unreasonable to assume that their music and culture is all borrowed from elsewhere. Rather than having this kind of one-sided relationship with other cultures and musics, the Roma are in fact an important point of exchange in a milieu in which music is shared, borrowed and reimagined from all sides.

But as we have seen, the notion of gypsy music is informed at least as strongly by perceptions of the gypsy figure as it is by studies of the music itself. Simon Frith has pointed out that in the definitions of specialist music charts, '"Women's music", for example, is interesting not as music which somehow expresses "women", but as music which seeks to define them, just as "black music" works to set up a very particular notion of what "blackness" is.'[32] Similarly, the idea of the gypsy musician is used to define the figure of the gypsy. But despite the renown of gypsy music and the contributions of Liszt and Bartók, very little has been written about it compared with the number of texts which deal with the Roma themselves.

The only book (other than this one) that purports to engage with the subject to the extent that it has the title *Gypsy Music* is by Hungarian musicologist Bálint Sárosi, and like the work of Liszt and Bartók, its main focus is on Hungarian music. Sárosi argues that gypsy music is not something that can be defined as a single distinct form:

The Gypsies have no common musical language, there is no common melodic treasury, or way of making music which is identical with all the Gypsies scattered throughout the world. So does Gypsy folk music exist at all? It does exist but it is generally different in every country, and everywhere it displays many features in common with local folk music.[33]

In one of the few books that provide an investigation concerning what gypsy music actually is, musicologist David Malvinni appears to take issue with this passage of Sárosi's: 'This statement would be an extremely offensive one for any Romani-rights advocate,' he says.[34] His concern is that to claim that the Roma have no unified style of music which crosses national borders is to deprive the Roma of a united identity as a people, and to imply that their music is simply a requisitioned form of non-Romani folk music. While this might be a worthy argument, we have seen (and as we continue to explore gypsy music we will see this to an even greater extent) that the stylistic elements of the music played by Romani people can vary quite substantially from place to place, and do share features with non-Romani folk musics.

As Malvinni goes on to say, 'The difficult task is to find a way of talking about Gypsy music that avoids both the potentially offensive innuendo of Sárosi, while not putting forth the idea that the Gypsy musical heritage is another repository among national repositories.'[35] It is necessary both for musical and political reasons to acknowledge that gypsy music does exist, but it must necessarily be defined in a different way, and perhaps with different reference points, to other folk musics, which are defined with reference to nation states. The distinction between Romani music and gypsy music, which allows for the possibility of both a music indigenous to the Roma and a hybridized form that may not have a strong connection to the Romani people, might be helpful in this regard. Certainly it would be preferable to the homogenizing narrative of the music industry, which unselfconsciously propagates a two-dimensional stereotype of gypsiness for the purposes of marketing that would be considered unacceptable in any other context and if any other minority group was its subject.

Even as stereotypes about the Roma are beginning to be broken down by activism and education, gypsy music remains an area in which they persist. Malvinni also points out that 'Roma musicians will sometimes revert to being eerily complicit in embodying Gypsiness, a stereotype that politically speaking should be rejected.'[36] Accordingly, Romani music as opposed to gypsy music might be under threat from being subsumed into the gypsy music category due to its association with gypsiness.

If we are seeking to identify a form of music that truly represents the Romani people of today then a good place to start might be the song 'Djelem Djelem', whose title translates as 'I travelled, I travelled', and which has been adopted as the anthem of the Roma. Numerous variations of the song exist and it has been performed and recorded by countless musicians. Although the music of 'Djelem Djelem' dates back to at least the late nineteenth century, many of the lyrics were composed by Romani activists around the time of the 1971 World Romani Congress, when it was adopted as the anthem of the Congress.

In practice, however, this emblematic song refuses the historical significance assigned to it by the Congress, retaining instead more of an emotional impact for most Roma rather than acting as a political rallying point. The notion that gypsy music has great emotional power and resonance is a familiar one, but in this case it is interesting that the emotional response comes from a Romani rather than a non-Romani audience.[37] It is arguable that this detail in itself is enough to justify the suggestion that 'Djelem Djelem' could be an example of Romani music rather than of gypsy music. However, it is perhaps not a universal enough song to be described in that way; Silverman notes that it was considered as a finale piece for the 1999 Gypsy Caravan tour, 'but the Spaniards and Rajasthanis had never heard of the song and the Romanians hardly knew it'.[38] The diversity and global spread of the Romani people is such that it is perhaps impossible for there to be a truly unifying Romani anthem.

A further problem is that this soulful and emotional song might be seen by non-Roma to represent the idea of gypsiness; the fact that it was mooted for performance in the Gypsy Caravan tour, an ensemble piece aimed at Western non-Romani audiences, is testament to this. Even if a music that is Romani rather than gypsy is identified, it is impossible to prevent it from being regarded as gypsy. Malvinni has noted that gypsy music 'appears stuck between reality and the imaginary – what Gypsies or "Roma" might play versus creative appropriation by composers'.[39] This appropriation can take numerous forms and moves in sometimes unexpected directions, and this is apparent in the ways in which Balkan Romani bands are marketed to the West.

3 GYPSY MUSIC AND BALKANISM

We have already addressed in some detail the negative perceptions that the Roma have suffered from, and the persecution that has derived from them. The word 'gypsy' has come to denote something more than simply the Romani people and must be negotiated carefully. Similarly, the word 'Balkan' must be negotiated with care, as the Balkan region, and its people, have also suffered from negative perceptions, and 'Balkan' has come to signify more than a region of southeastern Europe. Like the gypsy figure, the Balkans have been Othered.

Much Balkan music has long been thought of by Western listeners as gypsy music, even if it was neither performed nor informed by Romani musicians. Of course, neither Balkan music nor Romani music can be defined as a single entity: just as the music played by Roma in France differs from that performed by Roma in Spain or Hungary, the traditional musics of Serbia, Romania and Bulgaria also have their differences. It is true, however, that there are also similarities in the popular musics of Balkan countries, and since the end of the communist era they have had greater opportunities to influence one another. From the Western perspective, the differences are perhaps too subtle for listeners to identify, hence the conflation of Balkan and gypsy music by Western listeners.

What has long been widely regarded as gypsy music in the West is in fact distinct from any regional variations: on one hand what is thought to be gypsy music has been defined with reference to the Romungre music of Hungary which, as we have seen, has antecedents with Romani and non-Romani folk music, and has been influenced by the interpretations of classical composers. This form, played on string instruments with perhaps some accordion or woodwind, is associated with both gypsy musicians and with the Balkans, despite the fact that it is neither entirely connected to the Roma nor truly Balkan. But regardless of its actual geographical origin point, much of what is considered gypsy music more widely is also thought of as Balkan.

While gypsy music has been consumed enthusiastically in Western Europe for many years, music which is evidently Balkan but which is not produced or performed by Roma is received in a very different way. Indeed, this is a form of music that many in the West have learned to automatically ridicule before actually listening to it. An example of this is the derisive commentaries provided on UK broadcasts of the Eurovision Song Contest by former host Terry Wogan, which became an integral part of the show, and which, when deployed during entries from the Balkans, conformed to the views of the West. While people in the West are accustomed to seeing the Roma as excellent musicians, it is presumed that the inhabitants of Balkan countries who are not obviously gypsy will be significantly inferior: the region is considered to be comparatively underdeveloped in every aspect, and that extends as far as its music. What is not understood is that contemporary gypsy music in the Balkans – that is, the music played and listened to by Romani people – is not wholly distinct from the music of the non-Roma. Although Balkan Roma may play a form of music close to the usual Western approximation of gypsy music for non-Roma audiences, they are more likely to listen to music that has more contemporary pop and electronic influences.

Wogan's ribbing was never confined to the entries from the Balkans, and due to the typically low standard of British entries, it usually extended as far as the home team. However, a particularly anti-Balkan sentiment was visible in 2008, when the contest was held in Belgrade and interval entertainment was provided by Goran Bregović and his Weddings and Funerals Orchestra. For most of the nine-minute performance, Wogan talked over the music, keeping the sound turned well down, and at one point suggested that viewers might prefer to fetch refreshments than watch Bregović play. That was Wogan's last year as Eurovision host; he resigned complaining of political voting among Eastern European countries, so his antipathy towards Serbian music was probably not grounded entirely in the aesthetic, but his readiness to dismiss Balkan music was certainly apparent. However, this is not the sort of reaction that would normally be expected after a Bregović performance. He is well known in both Eastern and Western Europe for fusing the sounds of traditional Balkan music with those of rock and pop – in fact he composed Milan Stanković's 2010 Eurovision entry, 'Ovo Je Balkan'.

Bregović is also associated with gypsy music, and might be said to function as an intermediary between traditional gypsy music and pop and rock. Several famous Romani songs are known to Western audiences because they have been popularized by Bregović's arrangements. Having launched his musical career playing in rock bands in his native Bosnia, Bregović is now a composer of film music, best known for his collaborations with director Emir Kusturica. Kusturica is also a musician in his own right, and both his work and that of Bregović are worthy of examination here, as examples of music and film from within the Balkans that are familiar in the West, and which may contribute to commonly held Western perceptions of the region.

Bregović and Kusturica have similar backgrounds and their work has proved to be extremely compatible. They were both born in Sarajevo, and Kusturica has been described as 'a Bosnian

Goran Bregović and his Weddings and Funerals Orchestra performing in Cannes in 2007.

Muslim [who] has opted to stress the Serbian line in his origins',
while Bregović has also settled in Belgrade.[1] Kusturica's films may
deal with serious subjects, but they are typically colourful affairs,
and present the Balkans in a fashion that undoubtedly contributes
to the perceptions that persist today. In addition, they foster the
association between the Balkans and the gypsy. Romani characters
appear frequently; they are presented as leading madcap lives,
surviving on little with help from their ingenuity. The acrobatic
ruses of the gypsies combine effectively with Kusturica's

prominent inclusion of animals – which tend either to suffer comic misfortune or cause trouble for their human counterparts – and produce the atmosphere of a circus. This is in fact an effective analogy to describe how the Balkans are so often seen by the West: as being contained within a big top, which is full of comic chaos and characters both endearing and unsavoury.

Kusturica is also worthy of consideration here for his activity outside film-making, specifically his work as a musician. He joined the Serbian band Zabranjeno Pušenje (No Smoking) in the 1980s and, presumably in order to profit from his growing reputation and to increase their marketability in Anglophone countries, the group changed their name to Emir Kusturica and the No Smoking Orchestra. The band has significant followings in both Eastern and Western Europe, but although they are not Romani, they are thought of by many fans in the West as a gypsy music group and are often marketed as such, in an example of gypsiness being ascribed to a Balkan product. However, some critics have suggested that the No Smoking Orchestra is less authentic than many other Balkan gypsy music groups, with one describing the band as 'something like a poor man's version of Bregović's own Weddings and Funerals Band'.[2]

Kusturica has been making films since the early 1980s, but his breakthrough came in the early 1990s, when he began to receive greater exposure internationally. He achieved his greatest success in 1995 with *Underground*, for which he was awarded the Palme d'Or at Cannes. The film is a study of Yugoslavian history that is set over a period of half a century. This lengthy temporal span is mediated through the characters, whose lives are followed from the Nazi invasion of Belgrade in 1941 through to the conflict in Yugoslavia in the 1990s. Also following these characters is a brass band playing traditional gypsy music. This is the first of Kusturica's films in which we can observe the circus-like atmosphere that he is often associated with, and the music, replete with fast brass and jaunty gypsy tunes, is certainly suited to the circus. The music is often diegetic; bands of musicians appear on screen and follow the characters from scene to scene. This construction was repeated in Kusturica's 1998 comedy *Black Cat, White Cat*, which is set among a Serbian Roma community.

The close relationship between Kusturica's films and Bregović's music can be considered a possible reason for the association between gypsy music and the Balkans in the minds of Western consumers.[3] Moreover, the aesthetic of Kusturica's films can be seen in the way that Balkan gypsy music acts who play in the West present themselves.[4] This may be part of a trend for gypsy music to evolve according to the changing whims of its audiences; those non-Roma who have derived their impressions of the Roma from Kusturica's films will expect to see similar kinds of gypsies when they attend a concert of gypsy music. Bregović's music contributes significantly not only to these impressions of the gypsy, but also to perceptions of the Balkans.

Bregović has been accused of taking credit for the work of other musicians, and of being more a curator of Balkan and gypsy

Still from Emir Kusturica's *Black Cat, White Cat* (1998); the character of Zarije is freed from hospital with the aid of a gypsy music band.

Still from Emir Kusturica's *Underground* (1995); the musicians play on as a fight breaks out.

music than a composer.[5] Indeed, some of his best-known songs, such as 'Mesečina' and 'Ederlezi', are traditional pieces. But he has also been accused of appropriating the work of identifiable composers such as Serbian Romani singer Šaban Bajramović. With a repertoire that includes arrangements of traditional songs, along with his own compositions, he is little different from other performers of gypsy music, who draw on a particular body of music that is associated with gypsy musicians. But even if he is no plagiarist, it is easy to see how Bregović's work invites a potentially unfavourable reception, particularly when taken in conjunction with Kusturica's films.

In fact, the line between traditional songs and the compositions of specific individuals or groups can easily become blurred as folk music pieces and melodies travel and are recycled. Bregović has collaborated extensively with other musicians, some of whom are known for their associations with gypsy music: his album *Champagne for Gypsies* (2012) includes duets with artists such as the Gipsy Kings and Florin Salam, a performer of the contemporary Romanian style of *manele*. This example of

Bregović's work with other musicians might take the form
of a formalized set of collaborations, but it is a reminder that
musicians are continually working together within and around
the parameters of other styles.

A counterpoint to Bregović's collaborations and interpretations is Turkish singer Sezen Aksu's album *Düğün ve Cenaze*
(1997), which consists entirely of recordings of Bregović's songs.
While these are Bregović's original compositions, much of the
music is played by the Macedonian Roma brass band Koçani
Orkestar, and the album echoes the continuous exchange of
music between Romani and non-Romani peoples. Bregović's
position within gypsy music culture and canon indicates that new
connections and reinterpretations will always arise, and it is very
difficult to identify where engagement with tradition becomes
appropriation or plagiarism. The importance of tradition to the
idea of gypsy music means that this is even more the case with
gypsy music styles.

Balkan music is as indistinct an idea as gypsy music, and the
application of the term 'Balkan' to contemporary bands like
gypsy punks Gogol Bordello and indie folk group DeVotchKa
raises the question of what the word signifies, if it is not taken
to refer exclusively to the geographical area of the Balkans or
any of the countries that make up that region. This is addressed
by Maria Todorova in her book *Imagining the Balkans* (1997), in
which she examines how the Balkans have been perceived by
the West, and seeks to answer the question, 'How could a
geographical appellation be transformed into one of the most
powerful pejorative designations in history, international relations,
political science, and, nowadays, general intellectual discourse?'[6]
This is a persistent question. Why does 'Balkan' indicate not only
an area of southeastern Europe, but also a lack of civilization and
a tendency towards barbarism? Throughout the region's history

the Balkans have been stereotyped and the word has had a dual meaning since the early twentieth century, designating both the Balkan region itself and the stereotypes attached to it for centuries.[7]

Todorova introduces the term 'balkanism', which she relates to Said's notion of Orientalism, although there are distinctions between how the terms are used.[8] What connects the Balkans and the Orient is the fact that both are part of a network of easternness. Both are easterly regions, one in the global context, the other in the context of Europe. The Orient is seen as more eastern than Eastern Europe not only geographically but also culturally; similarly the Balkans are thought of as being more eastern than other parts of Eastern Europe, whether or not this is geographically the case, and certain areas of the Balkans are regarded as more eastern than others.[9] The association between balkanism and Orientalism is interesting, particularly when compared with how the Roma have been regarded. On some level, the Balkans function in the same way for the West, so it is unsurprising that the gypsy and the Balkans have become cultural bedfellows for Western onlookers and consumers.

But if the Balkans have been constructed as an idea as much as they have come about as a place, then we should briefly consider how this came about. Balkan history is relatively short; the term 'Balkan' only came into common use in the early nineteenth century, while most of the region was still part of the Ottoman Empire. The region is thought of as underdeveloped; the Balkans are seen as maintaining a level of civilization that is of those ages.[10] During this time, Ottoman control was weakening and some of the countries that we are familiar with today – Serbia, Bosnia-Herzegovina, Romania and Bulgaria – became independent states. This gave rise to the term 'balkanize', which denoted both a fragmentation into smaller states and a primitivization.[11]

The Ottoman Empire had always been regarded as non-European, and even as a threat to Europe and Christendom.

Its decline was therefore a relief to the powers of Western Europe. But while the Balkan countries that emerged from the Empire's ashes had in a way returned to Europe, they seemed to be tainted by their Ottoman past. They would become even more maligned after 28 June 1914, when Archduke Franz Ferdinand, the heir to the Austro-Hungarian throne, was assassinated in Sarajevo. The notion that there was a propensity for war in the Balkans and that the region's peoples were particularly prone to violence and barbarism was bolstered by the Balkan Wars of 1912 and 1913 and the assassination that became the most immediate cause of the First World War. This notion persisted throughout the interwar years and the Second World War, which saw both German and Soviet occupations in the Balkans.

Then, after 1945, by which time most Balkan countries were Soviet-controlled, the term 'Balkan' fell from usage. Now the region was simply part of Eastern Europe, all of which was seen as Other on account of its communist regimes, and the idea of the Balkans as an entity unto itself was forgotten.[12] But in the early 1990s the Balkans reappeared and once again became a concern of the West. As the countries tried to extricate themselves from their recent past, and to form stable governments that led them away from socialism and into capitalist Europe, there was further conflict. Reports of the atrocities that took place during the Balkan wars of the 1990s saturated the West; for many, these were shocking but not surprising, since the Balkans were infamous for bloody wars.

It has only been since the turn of the twenty-first century that the rest of Europe has begun to accept that the Balkans may be able to be included within its social and cultural borders. Slovenia became part of the European Union in 2004, along with several other Eastern and Central European countries, and Romania and Bulgaria followed in 2007. This development gave rise to the recent conception of the 'Western Balkans', used to describe

the countries that have not yet joined the EU: all of these countries
are expected to accede in the relatively near future. More recently,
Croatia became a member state in 2013.

Bearing in mind these developments, it does not seem inappro-
priate to echo Misha Glenny's questions regarding persistent
stereotypes, which he set out in 1999, but which remain pertinent
today:

> Why do so many Westerners shake their heads in laughter
> and despair at the Balkans? Why are the region's inhabitants
> seen either as congenitally irrational and bloodthirsty mobs,
> never happier than when they are slitting the throats of their
> neighbours, or as incompetent clowns in fanciful uniforms
> that mysteriously invoke a medieval past?[13]

Indeed, perceptions of the Balkans are so solidly codified in the
Western imagination that we can set out a set of stock characteristics that frequently recur. Firstly, the region is thought of as
being outside of Europe, and secondly, leading off from this point,
there is a lack of clarity concerning its geography and its borders.
Additionally, there is the widely held notion that the Balkans are
a particularly war-torn region; connected to this is the belief that
there is much corruption and amorality embedded in the area,
partially due to the communist legacy of the Balkans.

As we have seen, the Ottoman influence on the Balkans is
one reason why the region is considered to be beyond the strict
parameters of Europe. In short, the Balkans are commonly
regarded as geographically, but not culturally, European: this
is essentially a part of the discourse between East and West
that has resulted in Orientalism, hence Todorova's use of this
concept to inform her idea of balkanism. The Balkans are a
particularly significant region in that they have often been seen
as a bridge between Europe and Asia, and thus between East and

West.[14] They form a border region, separating the unknown and potentially dangerous East from the civilized West. Anything beyond the western edge of this borderland is thought to share the qualities of the East. However, East and West are not concrete here; the Balkan compass does not have fixed points. Todorova has noted that

> A Serb is an 'easterner' to a Slovene, but a Bosnian would be an 'easterner' to the Serb although geographically situated to the west; the same applies to the Albanians who, situated in the western Balkans, are perceived as easternmost by the rest of the Balkan nations.[15]

(One might add that a Rom would be considered an easterner to any of the above Balkan nationals, wherever in the world he or she happens to be.) The situation of Greece is also testament to this, as Todorova goes on to point out. Greece is generally not considered Balkan, even though it forms the tip of the peninsula, whereas its neighbours to the west and north, Albania and Bulgaria, are resolutely Balkan. It is as though the history of Greece, from its ancient civilization to its more recent functions as part of the EU and a member of NATO, has rendered it immune from becoming truly Balkan.

The accession to the EU of a number of Eastern European countries has done little to help the standard view of the Balkans. Although Romania and Bulgaria joined the EU in 2007, Albania and Moldova have yet to be admitted, and Slovenia and Croatia remain the only formerly Yugoslavian member states. This only heightens the differences between the Balkans and other regions of Eastern Europe. In addition, if EU membership is seen as necessary for Europeanness, then the Balkans remain outside. Conceptions of Europe are changing to reflect the growth of the EU but conceptions of the Balkans remain the same.

This position of being within Europe yet not quite European is mirrored in the position of European Roma. With roots in Rajasthan and their most significant populations in Eastern Europe, the Roma straddle Europe and Asia in their migratory history. The Balkans might geographically abut Asia, but the non-Europeanness of the region is a cultural demarcation – something that the region shares with the Roma.

The geography of the Balkans is unclear to many Western onlookers. In fact, there are also hierarchies of easternness within the Balkans, hierarchies which cannot necessarily be equated with the geography of the region, as Slavoj Žižek has pointed out:

> If you ask, 'Where do the Balkans begin?' you will always be told that they begin *down there*, towards the south east. For Serbs, they begin in Kosovo or in Bosnia where Serbia is trying to defend civilised Christian Europe against the encroachments of this Other. For the Croats, the Balkans begin in Orthodox, despotic and Byzantine Serbia, against which Croatia safeguards Western democratic values. For many Italians and Austrians, they begin in Slovenia, the Western outpost of the Slavic hordes.[16]

But the geographical uncertainty that is a feature of the Balkans is by no means confined to the demarcation of the region's borders. This position of not knowing quite where a country is, or being unable to pick it out on the page of an atlas, is one that is often alluded to when the region is being discussed. The fact that borders have tended to change and countries divide with comparative regularity is one reason for the confusion – indeed, this has given rise to the word 'balkanize', defined by the OED as, 'To divide (a region) into a number of smaller, often mutually hostile, political or territorial units,'[17] and which came into

common use in the 1920s following the demise of the Ottoman
Empire, the Balkan Wars and then the First World War.

Another issue that has caused a lack of thorough understanding about Balkan geography is the heterogeneity of many
countries there. Looking back as far as the ninth and tenth
centuries, there was a long-standing lack of homogenization
within the region, and the fragmentation of countries that
produced the term 'balkanize' may be an echo of an extant
topographical fragmentation; it is as though the natural geography of the region has made it difficult to form suitable borders
there.[18] The heterogeneity and instability associated with the
Balkans might have been exaggerated to some degree, but despite
this, the perception that heterogeneity is particularly widespread
exists, and this compounds the uncertainty of Balkan geography.[19]
From the perspective of the West, it is difficult not only to identify
Balkan countries, but also to determine who the inhabitants of
each of these countries are.

The process becomes more confusing still when the place
of the Roma is questioned, since they have no fixed homeland.
Indeed, this has caused such consternation that attempts have
been made to assign them to a particular place. Early activists
put forward the idea of 'Romanestan', a utopian state that the
Roma might inhabit as their own territory, and which might
be comparable with Israel. The idea of Romanestan was most
prominent in the 1930s, and was associated with the figure of
the gypsy king, a construct intended to give the Roma greater
credence among non-Roma. Various prominent Roma using the
title 'King of the Gypsies' sought to claim territory in Africa and
India.[20] However, the proposal of Romanestan was doomed to
failure, as there was insufficient unity amongst those attempting
to establish this country. In addition, the idea of a fixed and newly
created homeland for the Roma, even if it was one in which
they had greater autonomy, would be akin to the ghettoization

that they are already subjected to. The notion of relocating the Romani population to Africa certainly seems a dubious one in retrospect; it is somewhat reminiscent of the Nazi plan to relocate Europe's Jews to Madagascar.

In addition to changes on the geographical map, the shifting borders that exist between different countries commingle with those that exist between fiction and reality, with the result that countries which might have been thought of as fictions are sometimes reborn as actual places. This is often exploited by writers – the Transylvania of the Dracula myth, for example, is all the more sinister for being a place that is not quite real but not quite fictional. Although it is a real place, it is a region rather than a country, and its exact geography, history and politics are mysterious. A more recent example is the parodic travel guide *Molvanîa: A Land Untouched by Modern Dentistry* (2003), which also played on the uncertain geography of the region. Clearly a contraction of Moldova and Transylvania, its name is an example of the blur between fictional and actual places. Published in an almost identical format to recognizable travel guides such as *Lonely Planet* and *Rough Guides*, much of the humour in the book comes from the fact that one can imagine the uninformed believing that Molvanîa is a real place. It is also a good example of the way in which the Balkan region is often presented as a place that is rather risible, being comically undeveloped.

Caught up with the sense of an unknowable place that is exotic but inferior is the notion that the Balkans are a war-torn region; this is perhaps the most commonly held stereotype. Although the recent conflict in former Yugoslavia is the most obvious cause of this at present, it is by no means a recent perception. A 1909 book by William Howard-Flanders entitled *Balkania: A Short History of the Balkan States* turns out – though its title seems to suggest that the book will offer a general overview – to be little more than an account of the conquests

Molvanîa

Still
A LAND ∧ UNTOUCHED BY MODERN DENTISTRY

SANTO CILAURO, TOM GLEISNER & ROB SITCH

The funniest book about travel I have ever read... BILL BRYSON

Cover of Santo Cilauro, Tom Gleisner and Rob Sitch's *Molvanîa: A Land Still Untouched by Modern Dentistry* (10th anniversary edn, 2013).

and conflict that have occurred in the Balkans in the past two thousand years. Howard-Flanders concludes by declaring that more war is imminent, but that if the West becomes involved then it might be avoidable: 'A small match would suffice to set the whole Peninsula in flames, but the great hope of a peaceful solution is the love and peace shown by his most gracious Majesty Edward vii, whom may God long preserve!'[21] Although this account shows a rather unenlightened view of the relationship between the Balkans and Western Europe, this is typical of the era and, in fact, many more recent histories have tended to concentrate on conflict.

Sadly, Howard-Flanders was proved correct about the likelihood of war in the Balkans shortly after his book was published. The first Balkan War occurred in 1912–13 as a reaction to the control of the Ottoman Empire, and the second Balkan War, lasting little more than a month, in 1913. Soon afterwards, the First World War broke out, commencing with a declaration of war on Serbia by Austria-Hungary. It is important to note that this was an invasion from the West and that subsequent conflict within the Balkans involved Western armies; as such, it is difficult to argue that the people of the Balkans are particularly belligerent. Certainly, the involvement of the West has rarely served to extinguish any fires that had their roots in the region.

The notion of a region that is corrupt and amoral is closely related to the conception of a war-torn environment. This also results from embedded perceptions of the Balkan population as savage and uncivilized. Robert Bideleux and Ian Jeffries cite corrupt systems as hindrances to the recovery of the Balkans from the communist era.[22] They also speak of

the threat posed by the gangsterish, predatory and ostensibly 'ethnic nationalist' paramilitary movements which (once entrenched in power in particular localities) not only targeted former old neighbours transmogrified into 'enemies', but increasingly preyed upon 'their own people' as well by engaging in mafia-style protection rackets, drug-dealing, arms-smuggling, sex-slavery and people trafficking.[23]

While these activities have indeed caused problems in the Balkans, another problem is caused by repeated reference to the corruption that is so often presented as being inherent in the region. As we can see in the parody *Molvanîa*, a Western visitor to the Balkans might feel that they are at risk from thieves and con artists, and that they are in a place where corruption thrives.

However, this has become part of the allure of the Balkans: while the Orient has its exotic sexuality, the Balkan region is seen as a place with a looser sense of morality, where the police can be paid off with a packet of cigarettes and one might commit greater transgressions with impunity. Violence and corruption are so deeply associated with the region that these associations persisted even during the Cold War, when the term 'Balkan' was largely dormant, recurring only when stereotypically Balkan incidents occurred either in the Balkans or elsewhere. The assassination of the Bulgarian dissident Georgi Markov, who was killed with a poison-tipped umbrella in London in 1978, is a classic example.[24]

Although the Balkans were generally thought of as a part of communist southeastern Europe for almost half of the twentieth century, rather than as a distinct region, the current Western view of the Balkans is heavily informed by this period, with the region regarded as blighted by communist occupation. Of course, the actual situations varied from country to country and government to government: Tito's Yugoslavia, for example, was quite different to Ceauşescu's Romania. However, the commonly held Western view, which persists more than twenty years after the Cold War, is that the communist countries were very much alike.

Although the legacy of communism still affects perceptions of the Balkans, there have undoubtedly been improvements for the people of the Balkan countries since the fall of communism in Eastern Europe. But even though new political and social freedoms have been granted, the perceptions of the West do have an impact on how the people of post-communist countries perceive themselves, so these freedoms are not unqualified. Any detrimental effects that the legacy of communism continues to have on the inhabitants of the Balkans are in fact more likely to be the result of Western perceptions than of the recent history of the region.[25]

The situation of the Roma during the communist era was usually dictated by the drive towards assimilation. Those who still retained a nomadic lifestyle were in many cases encouraged or forced to settle in fixed homes, and in some cases were provided with work and housing. More oppressive measures such as displacement, the discouragement of the Romani language and even sterilization were also adopted in some Eastern European countries. For some Roma, however, living conditions improved considerably under communism; while they remained the subjects of disadvantage and victims of prejudice, many gained better housing, healthcare and incomes.[26]

While the Balkans might remain misunderstood in part due to the region's communist history, the Roma retain a pariah status that they have never been able to shed. Even if their lifestyles improved somewhat under communism, their marginalization was not overcome. Meanwhile, the association between the Roma and music persists. One striking example of gypsy music that addresses the communist period is the Taraf de Haïdouks song 'Balada Conducatorolui', which criticizes the dictatorship of Ceauşescu and mourns the deaths that occurred in the revolution that brought about his deposition. It's a subdued lament that serves as a reminder of how marginalized the voice of the Roma generally is, whatever the wider political situation.

In its best-known performance, 'Balada Conducatorolui' is played by Taraf de Haïdouks's former leader Nicolae Neacşu, who died in 2002, in Tony Gatlif's film *Latcho Drom* (1993). Accompanied by a cimbalom, Neacşu plays his violin using the technique of attaching a line of horsehair to the violin strings and pulling on the hair rather than using a bow: the resulting sound is a distinctive creaking that suits the dolour of the song. He describes Ceauşescu as a criminal, and sings of shortages of bread, cigarettes and power during his dictatorship. Although Ceauşescu was overthrown and Neacşu sings of freedom, the tone is sombre. This chimes with the paradox of gypsy identity and how gypsiness is perceived: while the gypsy is associated in the popular imagination with freedom, there are more complex positive and negative layers attached to this perception. Of course, similarly complex layers exist in the actual Romani experience and it is not surprising to find them reflected in gypsy music.

4 CONTEMPORARY GYPSY MUSIC
IN THE BALKANS

We know that gypsy music remains as indefinite a term as gypsy itself; the contemporary musicians whose music is considered to be gypsy vary widely. Wittgenstein's notion of family resemblances comes to mind here: although there may seem to be no particular common denominator that links certain styles of gypsy music, there is a resemblance between them.[1] However, this is not necessarily borne out solely through the way they sound. This will become evident as we consider three gypsy music bands from Romania. The strings of Taraf de Haïdouks may sound very different to the brass of Fanfare Ciocărlia, and the *manele*-influenced sound of Mahala Raï Banda is different again. What the three groups have in common is that they are all made up of Romani musicians, and all three play distinctive forms of music, all of which are marketed as gypsy music by record labels based in Western Europe.

In addition to being categorized as gypsy music, each of these bands can be thought of as world music. The world music genre was created in the late 1980s by record labels who sought a way of classifying music from non-Western or non-English-speaking cultures that was being marketed in the West.[2] If authenticity is important in popular music criticism, then it is all the more significant in discussions of world music. World music is widely thought of as a more authentic form of music than popular styles whose marketing machineries are more visible, and where songs are seen as sounding identical to each other; it provides an attractive contrast to the perceived inauthenticity of global mass media and offers something apparently more genuine.[3] Although the marketing behind world music is less apparent to Western consumers, the idea of the authentic is in fact used in the marketing process.[4] However, the exact parameters of the genre vary considerably: sometimes it is restricted to traditional forms of music, but it is often used to describe a fusion of Western and non-Western styles.

The world music genre has frequently been criticized for its generality; all music is world music, say some detractors. And there is no music that can be said to represent the whole world; although globalization is becoming an increasingly dominant phenomenon there is no single form of art or music that represents a sense of the global.[5] The term 'world music' has commercial rather than artistic purposes, since it is applied not to music that has a particular 'world music' sound but to a wide range of musics that are not already encapsulated in the music industry. We should note that styles presented as world music are not necessarily hidden from popular view in their home markets; while they might be little known in the West, they often have large popular audiences in their own regions, but are appropriated as new territory under the guise of world music.[6]

This will become significant when we consider the origins of three Romanian bands, and the ways in which they are represented, marketed and consumed in the West.

The musicians who make up Taraf de Haïdouks come from a village called Clejani, which has become regarded as an important centre of gypsy music. The village has historically been known as the home of many *lăutari*, the name given to professional Romani musicians. However, it is the more recent emergence of Taraf de Haïdouks that has consolidated the almost mythical repute of Clejani. Their music is string-led, dominated by violins and cimbaloms, and they are noted for their virtuosity and the astonishing speed with which they play. Writing about the music of the Hungarian Romungre, Carol Silverman has described how the 'essential ants'-nest bundle' that can be heard in the melody is played by more than one musician with different ornamentations applied.[7] The presence of such heterophony in the music of Taraf de Haïdouks only accentuates its pace. The clattering of their cimbaloms, which sound halfway between percussion and stringed instruments, and their frantic violin playing, together produce a sound that goes beyond the comparatively restrained *verbunkos* style while retaining the markers of gypsy music.

Taraf de Haïdouks are one of the best-known gypsy music bands in the West, playing regular tours in Western Europe and the United States; they can also boast that they have been flown to California by Johnny Depp to play at a party he was hosting. However, they do not have the same status in their native Romania. For example, at a major gypsy music concert in Bucharest in June 2009 they took on the role of support act, while the band at the top of the bill was the American gypsy punk band Gogol Bordello.

This might indicate that the Romanian audience for gypsy music is more interested in contemporary styles, while in the West there is a greater interest in traditional sounds and instruments. Such a hypothesis is supported by David Malvinni's comparison of the receptions in Romania of Taraf de Haïdouks and the *manele* singer Adrian Copilul Minune. *Manele* is a contemporary urban style of music, connected to the gypsy music tradition insofar as it is performed by Romani musicians, but it is primarily electronic, with synthesizers and drum machines used extensively.

Writing in 2002, Malvinni describes Minune's cassettes as hugely popular in Bucharest.[8] Taraf de Haïdouks, on the other hand, are less well known in Romania. This is not simply because there is no interest in their music, Malvinni argues. He cites a lack of promotion on the part of their management, prohibitively high concert prices by Romanian standards, and the fact that their music was sold only on CD rather than cassette tapes (which remained the standard popular format for distributing music in Romania in the early 2000s) as explanations for this. In other words, they are a gypsy music band aimed squarely at Western audiences.

Although the appeal of Taraf de Haïdouks in the West is largely to do with a presumed sense of tradition, their music is in fact different to, and more modern than, the music played in Clejani in the 1960s. Arguably, the band is losing its authenticity

Taraf de Haïdouks.

as a gypsy music group as it shifts its sound from heterophonic *verbunkos* and the sense of tradition implicit in that style to something that has been modernized in order to keep up with the demands of world music and its audiences.[9] The association with tradition is still important to the presentation of Taraf de Haïdouks, but as we will see, elements of fusion have been important to their enduring success. The fact that Taraf de Haïdouks are not only Romani musicians playing for non-Roma, but also musicians from Eastern Europe playing to the West, is also significant. Exoticized due to both their gypsiness and their Balkan origins, they have a dual appeal in the West.

Of course, their popularity in the West is due to more than a Western fascination with traditional gypsy music; deliberate marketing efforts are also involved. While the name Taraf de Haïdouks, which means 'band of brigands', might connote a group of musicians brought together by chance who operate outside the mainstream, this is a carefully fabricated image, for they are in fact a manufactured band. This term most immediately calls to mind pop groups assembled by record labels and might seem to diminish the authenticity of the music of Taraf de Haïdouks. The musicians are in fact steeped in a long-standing musical tradition, but like any number of Western boy bands, the group as it is constituted for touring in the West was manufactured by a promoter.[10] Their story begins when 'In 1986 musicologist Speranţa Rădulescu took a Swiss colleague, Laurent Aubert, to Clejani. Aubert recorded a six-man band and arranged for Ocora, an ethnographic label funded by Radio France, to release a CD in 1988.'[11] The resulting album, *Roumanie – Musique des Tsiganes de Valachie* inspired Belgian music promoter Stéphane Karo to seek out Clejani. He succeeded, and promised the *lăutari*, who were deprived of movement under Ceauşescu, that he would take them to Belgium:

Karo kept his word: on hearing of Ceauşescu's execution in 1989, he returned to Clejani and assembled a dozen Lăutari, lead [sic] by [Nicolae] Neacsu. He named the outfit Taraf de Haïdouks (Band of Outlaws) and signed them to the Belgian label Crammed Discs. Their 1991 debut, *Muzique des Tziganes de Roumanie* was an immediate sensation, topping the European world music charts.[12]

This process follows the well-established precedent of Romani musicians playing music for a non-Romani audience. However, the distance between musician and listener has a new dimension here, as the 'band of gypsies' has been assembled by a non-Roma from the West. This shows how the musical relationship between the Roma and non-Roma has changed, and also suggests that perceptions of what constitutes gypsy music are so engrained that it can be constructed by the non-Roma who want to hear it. Taraf de Haïdouks clearly conform to the West's expectations of gypsy music and, despite their enormous skill and status as the pre-eminent modern *lăutari*, their renown depends on their gypsiness as much as on their musicianship.

This is certainly not a criticism of their success, nor an attempt to cast doubts on their talents. In fact, it is their remarkable skill as musicians that gives rise to their perceived gypsiness. Although Taraf de Haïdouks are Roma, this is less important in the West than the fact that they are gypsies, and this is determined by their musicianship as much as it is by their ethnicity. However, this status of gypsiness is maintained not only by the band's virtuosity, but also by their repertoire. In order to remain successful in the West, it is necessary for gypsy music bands to introduce novel aspects to their sound, whilst maintaining the close tie to tradition that is expected of gypsy musicians.

Taraf de Haïdouks' 2007 album *Maskarada* is an interesting example of how novelty and tradition can be combined.

Maskarada consists predominantly of renditions of classical works played in a gypsy music style, along with a few original compositions. It is presented as an example of 're-gypsyfication', whereby the classical pieces that were informed by traditional gypsy music are reclaimed by Romani musicians and reinterpreted in a more outwardly gypsy style. The composers covered include the Hungarians Béla Bartók and Joseph Kosma, as well as Spanish composers such as Isaac Albéniz and Manuel de Falla, whose presence invites us to think of flamenco. *Maskarada* reopens the debate about gypsy music that was instigated by Liszt, and, as might be expected of a band whose gypsiness is used as a marketing tool, the view taken by their record label is that gypsy music was borrowed from Roma by non-Roma, rather than the other way around. However, the overall message given on the CD sleeve is more balanced than Liszt's:

> In the early twentieth century, many composers drew their inspiration from national folklore, often borrowing from Roma musicians to create their own vision of an exotic and largely imaginary Orient. Things have now been turned around, as one of the world's leading Gypsy bands have taken hold of classical pieces and have 're-gypsyfied' them, giving them an exhilarating make-over.[13]

So *Maskarada* purports to function as a reclamation of a music that has its earliest origins with the Roma. However, the author of the liner notes admits that the association between the two forms of music is ambiguous:

> As a result of the constant to-and-fro, it is not easy to decide who is wearing the disguise: is it the rural Gypsy band playing a Strauss waltz, or the Western European orchestra playing in a 'Hungarian' style? It's a gigantic masquerade.[14]

This is a refreshing way of looking at gypsy music; it allows us to see it as something that can have a reciprocal relationship with other styles, even though it does not offer any answers as to whether there can be a definitive gypsy music. In *Maskarada*, Taraf de Haïdouks are perpetuating the exchange between gypsy music and classical music that has gone on for well over a hundred years, showing that even though there is no current trend for classical composers to utilize gypsy elements, the relationship nonetheless persists. More significantly, it suggests that Romani musicians maintain an awareness of music from beyond their traditional gypsy repertoires. Even if this is in fact the work of their management, it means that they appear as less of a closed culture and are less open to stereotyping.

The albums subsequently released by Taraf de Haïdouks, who remain signed to the Crammed Discs label, demonstrate how notions of authenticity can easily be redefined in a short space of time. Their 2011 album *Band of Gypsies 2* was a collaboration with Macedonian Romani brass band Kočani Orkestar, which bound together two distinct styles of music under the amorphous term of gypsy music, arguably diluting the distinct heritages of the *lăutari* and the brass band into a single semblance of tradition. On the other hand, their 2015 album *Of Lovers, Gamblers and Parachute Skirts* – its title sounding as though it could be the name of a Kusturica film in the way it summons up the colour of the imagined Balkans – was presented as a return to the band's roots. As we have seen, however, the immediate roots of Taraf de Haïdouks are not quite as deep as they might appear.

If Taraf de Haïdouks are regarded in the West as a prime example of contemporary gypsy music, then they have a counterpart in Fanfare Ciocărlia, a Romani brass band who have been successfully exported to Western Europe. Indeed, they have much in common with Taraf de Haïdouks: although their music is played on brass

The Vladica Novković orchestra from Zagužanje, southern Serbia, at the Guča Trumpet Festival in 2016.

rather than string instruments, it is also characterized by its fast tempo and the dexterity of the musicians, who maintain the pace while playing complex melodies. More so, however, Fanfare Ciocărlia share their style with numerous other bands, and can be classified as part of a subgenre of gypsy music known sometimes as gypsy brass, sometimes as Balkan brass. As we have seen, the term Balkan is frequently misused, and Balkan countries are subject to generalizations, but the term Balkan brass seems in a way to be apposite, since the music is not confined to any one part of the region. Other brass bands who have been imported to the West include the Macedonian Kočani Orkestar, and the Boban Marković Orkestar from Serbia. The Guča festival, already discussed, is the predominant showcase of the style, and testifies to the sheer number of musicians playing Balkan Brass music.

On the other hand, Balkan brass is something of a misnomer, since its origins lie outside the Balkans: it derives from Ottoman military music and is an example of the legacy of Ottoman rule in the Balkans. As will be apparent from its origins, Balkan brass is

Marko and Boban Marković.

not an exclusively Romani form of music. However, the bands who have achieved the greatest success playing it for Western audiences tend to be Romani, and it is presented to such audiences as a form of gypsy music. This is a reflection of the fact that Balkan music and gypsy music are often incorrectly conflated. Any music that originates in the Balkans is often thought to be gypsy music, and much of the music produced by Romani musicians is regarded as Balkan. Indeed, Gypsy brass has come to be a synonym for Balkan brass in the same way that gypsy music and Balkan music almost are synonymous terms in the West.

The popularity that Fanfare Ciocărlia enjoy in the West is not the only thing they have in common with Taraf de Haïdouks. They are also from a small Romanian village, Zece Prăjini in the northeast of the country, and have a similar career trajectory to the *lăutari* of Clejani, and a similar myth of origin. In the same way that Taraf de Haïdouks were manufactured by Belgian promoters, Fanfare Ciocărlia were manufactured by a German, Henry Ernst, who heard about the brass musicians of Zece Prăjini in 1996 while travelling in Romania. He says of his visit to the village:

> It was so amazing I ended up staying not one day but three months and assembling a brass band. Fanfare is a French word that's passed into Romanian and is used to describe a brass band. Ciocărlia, that's the Romanian for a lark's song. I returned to Germany and sold everything I had to make one tour.[15]

Ioana Szeman has described such accounts of Western managers importing music from the Balkans as 'discovery narratives that re-enact Balkanism', and it is apparent that the romance of these stories contributes to the popularity of the musicians in the West.[16] Although Fanfare Ciocărlia's initial tour was not a financial success, the reception that they achieved convinced Ernst to turn them professional and he founded a record label, Asphalt Tango. Fanfare Ciocărlia are now highly successful, touring internationally and continuing to gain great acclaim. Asphalt Tango has also grown, having released not only eight Fanfare Ciocărlia albums, but also records by other popular Romani musicians from the Balkans, such as Mahala Raï Banda and Kal; the label now styles itself 'the leading voice in Gypsy and Eastern music'.

Although the word 'Balkan' is conspicuously absent from that self-description, hidden between the romantic associations of the gypsy figure and the long-standing Orientalism of the East, Szeman's point about balkanism is pertinent here. The Balkans are presented as if they have an enhanced capacity to conceal previously unheard music, and the fact that this hidden music is played by Romani musicians compounds the sensation: the mystique of the gypsy figure is such that the gypsy might be expected to conceal elements of musical tradition. It is up to the Western traveller, however, to uncover these secrets of gypsy music and present them to a wider audience. In this context, the similarities in the discovery narratives of Fanfare Ciocărlia and Taraf de Haïdouks are truly striking; and ironically, in their similarity the two stories cancel out the sense of novelty that each is intended to elicit. Meanwhile, the quasi-colonial aspects of these narratives require almost no unpacking.

Like Taraf de Haïdouks, Fanfare Ciocărlia – or more likely their management – have sought to introduce novel aspects into their sound so as to maintain their marketability to Western audiences. Their 2005 album *Gili Garabdi: Ancient Secrets of Gypsy Brass* starts with the premise that a connection can be drawn between gypsy music and jazz:

'How many Gypsies fled Romania when slavery ended for the United States?' Ioan [Ivancea, Fanfare Ciocărlia's former bandleader, who died in 2006] once answered when asked if jazz was a big influence on Fanfare. 'Who's to say our cousins who went to the U.S. didn't help invent jazz?'[17]

Garth Cartwright, who wrote the sleeve notes for that album, seems taken with this idea, noting in his book *Princes Among Men* (2005) that 'Tens of thousands of Balkan Roma migrated to the U.S. during the nineteenth century' and that 'the Roma would have lived – as they did in the Balkans – in the poor part of town, cheek by jowl with another people who knew too much about slavery and discrimination and used brass and string

Fanfare Ciocărlia performing live.

instruments.'[18] Although gypsy jazz became an established form in Paris from the 1930s onwards, this jazz connection seems a rather doubtful possibility and, in fact, the music of *Gili Garabdi* is not all that dissimilar from any of Fanfare Ciocărlia's previous work, which was presented as straight-up gypsy brass, connected to the traditions of Balkan Roma rather than to the African American pioneers of jazz. Compared to their earlier albums there is a slight increase in the number of slower pieces, and at times the use of guest vocalists helps to make the jazz connection seem more credible: for example, Bulgarian Roma singer Jony Iliev, an extremely versatile vocalist, lends a mellow croon to 'Ma Maren Ma' that would not sound out of place on a smooth jazz record. But the insistent pulse of the tenor horns that is characteristic of gypsy brass underlies much of the album, and these bass lines alone make the record far more gypsy than jazz.

One attempt at foregrounding the jazz premise is a cover of Duke Ellington's 'Caravan'. This is an almost unrecognizable version of Ellington's original, and while the Fanfare Ciocărlia interpretation swings in the same way, the tempo is increased to the level typically used by the Roma, and the tenor horns provide their usual bass line. A similarly unrecognizable cover version of Steppenwolf's 'Born to Be Wild' features on Fanfare Ciocărlia's subsequent album *Queens and Kings* (2007). But while 'Born to Be Wild' makes no claims to represent a connection between gypsy music and hard rock, 'Caravan' is intended as evidence for the supposed link between gypsy music and jazz. But the striking difference between Fanfare Ciocărlia's version and Duke Ellington's original destroys the likelihood of this link, reinforcing the gypsiness of the music and denying its jazz connections. While this may be great music, it is not jazz.

Overall, *Gili Garabdi* is more successful in concept than realization: the dubious suggestion that Romani émigrés may have helped to invent jazz in America is more original than the music presented to illustrate this idea. However, as with Taraf de Haïdouks's *Maskarada*, it suggests that Romani musicians are interested in experimenting with genre. Even if such fusions are instigated by the musicians' management, this may help to free them from stereotyping, with Western consumers being invited to consider the history of the Romani people, and how it connects with the histories and musics of other cultures.

The next collaboration Fanfare Ciocărlia were involved in raises quite different questions. The 2014 album *Devil's Tale* was recorded with the Canadian guitarist Adrian Raso, and in its mixture of brass and strings, it could be compared to the collaboration between Taraf de Haïdouks and Koçani Orkestar. However, there is a distinct difference. Raso is not Romani – he is influenced in part by gypsy jazz, but this is one precedent among many to be heard in his work – and *Devil's Tale* is perhaps less a gypsy music record than a world music fusion album. Raso is credited with composing and arranging all of its tracks, and the Romanians are given second billing to him on the album sleeve and for the most part provide an accompanying role behind his solo guitar playing. Despite being 'the leading voice in Gypsy and Eastern music', Asphalt Tango do not use the term 'gypsy music' in the publicity around the album. Compare this with their spiel for a collaborative album involving Fanfare Ciocărlia and the Serbian brass band Boban and Marko Marković Orkestar: 'Finally, the two titans of East European Gypsy music go head to head in a Balkan brass encounter of epic proportions.'[19]

The stylistic elements of the album are numerous. The title track has a sound that is more like surf guitar than anything else, while 'The Absinthe-minded Gypsy' does recall Balkan music, sounding not unlike much of the work of Goran Bregović. The song titles are telling, evoking genres of music and arguably planting associations in the listener's head before they have even heard the music. 'Spiritissimo' is a meaningless word, but it

Fanfare Ciocărlia performing live.

evokes Southern Europe in its Italian sound, and the track that carries that name is a flamenco-influenced piece. 'C'est la Vie', with its easy-to-comprehend French title, is informed by gypsy jazz. 'The Absinthe-minded Gypsy' is slightly more complex in its signification; it is the only title to use the word 'gypsy', as if to remind us of Fanfare Ciocărlia's usual presentation as a gypsy music band, but 'absinthe' calls to mind Parisian nightlife in the heyday of Django Reinhardt. The use of a pun is a reminder that the album is marketed predominantly to an Anglophone audience; the Romanian Romani musicians are playing for non-Romanian non-Roma.

It is to be assumed that, as was the case with Taraf de Haïdouks and *Maskarada*, *Devil's Tale* was conceived by Fanfare Ciocărlia's management. Again, we find a situation in which the Romani musicians have a passive role in a negotiation in which non-Romani actors assume a dominant position. In this case the implications are more troubling still: the Roma are playing in support of a non-Romani musician who is using elements of their music to define his own sound. On the other hand, we have previously discussed the desire expressed by some rural Balkan Romani musicians to move to the city in search of more lucrative employment opportunities; and in a way the widespread success and transnational, trans-genre collaborations of bands like Fanfare Ciocărlia are an extension of this kind of move, executed with the support of non-Roma.

A further question that *Devil's Tale* raises is the possibility that there are hierarchies of gypsy music. Gypsy jazz, which has its origins in Western Europe, is perhaps higher up the hierarchy than the gypsy music of the Balkans: there is greater distance between gypsy jazz and the Romani people, so it is easier to market the genre in a conventional way. The role of tradition and authenticity is another factor: the brass of Fanfare Ciocărlia is less established as a gypsy music than the string-led music of Taraf de Haïdouks, which can be traced back to the *verbunkos* tradition. Accordingly, there is less to be gained from pitching Taraf de Haïdouks alongside a Western, non-Romani guitarist. This concern with tradition will remain important as we go on to consider a third Romanian gypsy music band, Mahala Raï Banda.

As is the case with Taraf de Haïdouks, Fanfare Ciocărlia are more popular in the West then they are in their native country. The final Romani band from Romania that I want to consider is unusual in being a crossover artist in terms of their popularity in both the Balkans and the West. The idea of the crossover artist, which is used to describe musicians who have audiences in more than one genre or region, is not exclusive to world music, but is frequently linked to it. While Mahala Raï Banda are popular in their native Romania, their music has also been successfully exported to the

West. This kind of crossover places them within a tradition of crossing over in gypsy music, which has been avidly consumed by both Romani and non-Romani audiences for centuries.

Mahala Raï Banda do not have the rural associations and discovery narrative of Taraf de Haïdouks or Fanfare Ciocărlia, nor the connection to long-standing musical tradition. The Romanian word *mahala* means 'slum' and is generally used to refer to the Romani ghettos on the fringes of cities,[20] and Mahala Raï Banda are indeed a more urban band, and play the more urban style of *manele*, which is very popular, although divisive, in Romania, but little known in Western Europe.

Cristina Mosora has described *manele* as:

> a musical genre that mixes the local Gypsy and oriental beats with cheap synthesizers in explicit, bad grammar songs about love, sex, money and enemies. It is an urban 'dirty' popular music closely related to the Bulgarian chalga and the Serbian turbo folk and it is played exclusively at the moment by interpreters of Roma origin.[21]

Manele is an indigenous product made in the Balkans for a Balkan audience, and it is primarily produced by Romani musicians. However, as is the case with the ostensibly Balkan style of brass music, its origins lie with the Ottoman Empire. It was later taken up by *lăutari* and became an urban form by that means before evolving into its current style.[22] In its current form, *manele* has been influenced by Western music, including rock, electronica and hip-hop.[23]

This marks a continuation of the two-way exchange of musical styles that has gone on between Romani musicians and those of the regions in which they have settled. *Manele* has been influenced by Ottoman music, has gone on to inform Balkan beats in Western Europe, and has also taken on rap and hip-hop

Mahala Raï Banda performing live in 2010.

influences. The difference between this evolution and that of earlier gypsy music is that Romani musicians now no longer have to travel to a particular region to hear its music. Due to the increased availability of recordings, which has come about as a result of technological developments and the end of communist control of music consumption, Romanian Roma have been able to listen to and draw upon hip-hop from New York or Los Angeles without ever leaving the Balkans. Equally, the fact that musicians in the West have had increased access to Balkan music has no doubt contributed to the development of new styles of music.

Manele is controversial in Romania; although it has a wide following, it also has many detractors, and it was prohibited during the communist era due to its Romani associations. Today, its ambiguous reception has much to do with its context as a gypsy form of music; it acts as a form of counterculture in that it was once banned, and in its associations with both gypsy music and with Western styles. While it is popular with many young Romanians, older and more educated people are more likely to be detractors, since *manele* is seen as distanced from both Romanian culture and more desirable Western cultures.[24]

This appeal of subversion is very similar to the allure that is associated with gypsy music in the West; however, *manele* is not a style of music that has achieved popularity outside of the Balkans. The music that Mahala Raï Banda play is closer to that of most contemporary Balkan Roma musicians than anything else that has been successfully imported to the West, but as Garth Cartwright explains:

> Mahala Raï Banda's manele flourishes only hint at the electronic hybrids developing in the Balkans. 'Mahala' means 'Gypsy ghetto' and in these urban environments, digital technology is employed to make music. Most of this music will never leave the Balkans; it's just too trashy and bizarre for Western audiences to get their heads around.[25]

The story of how Mahala Raï Banda came to be known in the West differs somewhat from the discovery narratives that accompanied the first recordings of Fanfare Ciocărlia and Taraf de Haïdouks. However, they are connected to both of these bands, and can be thought of almost as a gypsy music supergroup, which draws on and updates the trends established by already popular gypsy music bands. Mahala Raï Banda is led by Aurel Ioniță, a musician from Clejani, who is related to several members of Taraf de Haïdouks: this is undoubtedly an important detail in the marketability of the band. In addition, the group includes brass musicians from Zece Prăjini, the village from which Fanfare Ciocărlia were recruited.

However, their music is not simply an amalgam of the *lăutari* and brass styles in the same way that the collaboration between Taraf de Haïdouks and Kočani Orkestar is; it also takes on other sounds, not only the *manele* that drives it, but also styles from outside the Balkans and the traditional gypsy music repertoire. Their 2009 song 'Balkan Reggae', for example, is more or less what its title suggests: a piece of reggae music played by a Balkan band. As we have previously identified, they are a consciously more urban band, and they are presented as being more closely aligned with the absorbent, multicultural values of the contemporary city than with the sense of tradition that is explicit in the presentation of most other Balkan gypsy music bands.

This is a valuable selling point for their work, and is an alternative to the discovery narrative. However, Mahala Raï Banda are also subject to a discovery narrative; the difference is that this is not made public in the same way that the narratives connected to Fanfare Ciocărlia and Taraf de Haïdouks are. They are marketed as having been formed by Ioniţă in Bucharest, and this is technically true, but they were initially founded as an earlier band, Rom Bengale, which collapsed due to addiction problems.[26] The first album released under the Mahala Raï Banda name, a self-titled record from 2004, was on the Crammed Discs label – the same label that brought Taraf de Haïdouks to prominence in the West. Their two subsequent albums have been released on Asphalt Tango, the label founded in order to promote Fanfare Ciocărlia. Evidently there is an implicit discovery narrative attached to Mahala Raï Banda.

This narrative is hidden in part by the fact that the band has an audience both in the West and in the Balkans. They are a group through whom *manele* can be marketed to Western gypsy music audiences as an exotic new form of gypsy music, more authentic in the contemporary urbanized age, due to their city origins; but their music is sufficiently Westernized in its style that it is regarded as having worth in Balkan communities. There is a double irony here. A more Western-sounding style of music has more value to Balkan audiences despite the sense of tradition that Western promoters associate with the Balkans in order to promote gypsy music – and to some degree this is the case with Mahala Raï Banda, whose connections to Clejani and Zece Prajini are presented as being important. Yet because their music is consumed within the Balkans, they are arguably a more authentic form of Balkan gypsy music than *lăutari* or brass bands.

In fact, this could be said of *manele* more broadly, and such an argument has been made by Romanian writer Adrian Schiop, who

> considers manele one of the most authentic musical movements to emerge in Romania, being much more authentic than, say Romanian hip-hop, which can be perceived as one of the symbols of the 'self-colonisation' of Romanians, avidly adopting Western models of modus operandi without critical reflection.[27]

Authenticity is significant here in the context of world music, which as we have seen is treated as a form of music in which authenticity is essential. But we also know that the device of world music has been used as a means of appropriating popular music styles from outside of the Western commercial mainstream. So *manele* is authentic in the sense that it has been presented as such as a form of world music. It might also be as authentic as a form of Romanian music listened to in Romania, but its authenticity is more important to those consuming from outside as they discover *manele*.

If Romanian hip-hop is an example of self-colonization by Romanians, then more traditional Balkan gypsy music can be regarded as having been colonized by non-Roma from outside the Balkans. This is apparent in the way in which the management of Taraf de Haïdouks and Fanfare Ciocărlia have exerted power over the bands by manipulating the histories of the musicians. Although this is the case to some degree with Mahala Raï Banda, the power dynamic is less pronounced, since the band has a greater audience in its native Romania and is thus tied less tightly to its Western audiences.

Manele is both a rural and an urban form, and Romani listeners form much of its audience.[28] The distinction between rural and urban has been important as we have examined various styles of gypsy music, so it is striking to come across a type of gypsy music that straddles the boundaries between city and countryside. To encounter a gypsy music with a large Romani audience is more striking still, since the notion of what gypsy music is has historically been dictated by non-Roma. In addition, the success of Mahala Raï Banda in the West indicates that there is potential for *manele* to be accepted as a form of gypsy music. The Romanian form of *manele* has counterparts in other Balkan countries: turbo-folk in Serbia, *chalga* in Bulgaria and *tallava* in Albania. There are subtle differences between these forms, but the merging of electronic and folk elements is key to them all, and all are connected to Romani communities. These are perhaps the closest forms of music to an archetypal gypsy music that we can identify today: connected to tradition, yet thoroughly modern; both rural and urban; and listened to by Roma and non-Roma alike.

This is indicative of a sense of hybridity in contemporary gypsy music. Such hybridity has been apparent in gypsy music for many years – the arguments posited by Liszt and Bartók about how far Romani musicians were informed by non-Roma, and vice versa, are evidence of this – but it is arguable that there is now a more conscious hybridity in both gypsy music and its audiences.

Poster from the 2009
Balkanfest in Kiev.

The fact that Taraf de Haïdouks and gypsy punk band Gogol
Bordello appeared on the same billing in Bucharest reveals that
two quite different styles of music, when juxtaposed beneath
the gypsy music umbrella, can share an audience. This was also
apparent at the Balkanfest festival, which took place in Kiev in
December 2009. The line-up included Fanfare Ciocărlia, Gogol
Bordello and four other bands from opposite ends of the 'gypsy'
music spectrum: Koçani Orkestar, Serbian Romani rock band Kal,
Ukrainian ska band Haydamaky and Emir Kusturica's band, the
No Smoking Orchestra.

The name 'Balkanfest' should not go unremarked here;
although more than half of the musicians involved were from
the Balkans, the festival itself took place in Ukraine, and the
music was not exclusively Balkan. As such, we can see an

instance of balkanism taking place in a location that is, from a Western perspective, beyond the Balkans. The gypsy music being performed here is taken as indicative of the nature of that region; while notions of the Balkans as war-torn or uncivilized were not present here, the stereotype of wildness and hedonism that the region shares with the Roma was very much in evidence.

However, the Balkans are not the only part of Europe to have a gypsy music tradition that has gained popularity outside its home region. Gypsy music styles from elsewhere in Europe, such as Russian gypsy music, flamenco and gypsy jazz, might sound quite different to those from the Balkans, but there are similarities in the dynamic of their performance, with Romani musicians playing for non-Roma, and in the concern with authenticity, tradition and the exoticized figure of the gypsy that is attached to them. As we go on to explore these styles we will also see that the Balkans are not the only place in Europe that has been mythologized from outside.

5 GYPSY MUSIC IN RUSSIA

Gypsy music from Russia is arguably the most popular and well-known gypsy music after that from the Balkans. As with Balkan gypsy music, it cannot be defined according to a single sound or style; rather it encompasses a range of styles. The concept of a Russian gypsy music, and indeed that of a Russian music more generally, has been homogenized not only through popular perception, as is the case in the Balkans, but also as a consequence of the Soviet era, when music was expected to conform to the model of a state-sponsored music that was deemed representative of Soviet culture. As a result, what is considered Russian gypsy music has been strongly influenced by external factors, and might therefore be regarded as less authentic as a form of Romani music. But even if its attachment to Romani traditions is not authentic, this form of Russian gypsy music was created with the image and perceived traditions of the gypsy figure in mind, and as such should be regarded as a gypsy music.

Before the Russian Revolution of 1917, gypsy music in Russia was perhaps closer to the authentic traditions of Russian Roma, but it was still moulded to the expectations of non-Romani audiences. The form of gypsy music performance that has historically been regarded as the most prestigious in Russia was the gypsy choir, and subsequently the gypsy theatre, and occupations within these establishments gave Roma the opportunity to increase their social status. Gypsy choirs, in which

Roma sang popular Russian folk songs, usually accompanied by guitars, were popular from the late eighteenth century; their popularity peaked around the 1830s, but they continued well after this time.[1] The repertoire of the choirs was originally derived from Russian folk music, and the Romani performers sung in Russian, but over time the songs were refashioned and embellished by the Roma and sometimes sung in Romani. In this way, the music underwent a process of becoming gypsy music.

The gypsy choir was important in bringing greater social mobility to Roma, as singing was the only occupation that allowed Roma to settle in urban areas. In the countryside, meanwhile, choirs of Romani serfs were formed on estates.[2] One noted choir was founded in this way by A. G. Orlov in 1774; its performers were freed from serfdom in 1807 and permitted to settle in Moscow.[3] In time, gypsy choir dynasties were established, with generations of the same families continuing to perform in choirs and coming to be regarded as a kind of elite.[4]

The pattern of Roma performing for non-Roma, which we have already seen examples of in the Balkans, is also apparent in the case of the choirs, and this can be interpreted as an extension of the servitude from which the choirs derived. Additionally, there was an expectation from non-Roma about how the Romani singers should appear: when some adopted the usual dress of the Russian upper classes, there were complaints from audiences that they did not look like gypsies, and so some choirs deliberately styled themselves to appear more like stereotypical gypsies. However, the choirs did give Roma greater visibility and status in Russian society, along with more autonomy: some, including Orlov's choir, had Romani directors.[5] Music thus became a pathway to prosperity and, significantly, a level of assimilation; the romance associated with the gypsy offered tangible benefits for those Roma who acknowledged and played up to it.

This assimilation, which was not achieved by all Russian Roma, was a slow process. The first Roma to arrive in Russia did so in the fifteenth century, later than the earliest arrival of Roma in the Balkans. It is likely that some made their way to Russia by way of the Balkans and then Ukraine, while others migrated through northern Europe and Poland. By the time of the late eighteenth century some were assimilated into Russian society to the extent that a Romani intelligentsia was in evidence in the cities of Moscow and St Petersburg, and music was a key vehicle for this. Meanwhile, many Roma in rural areas were seen as backward, and subject to greater persecution. The divide between urban and rural Roma that we have already encountered elsewhere was thus particularly pronounced in Russia, and the greater status afforded to some urban Roma in Russia was a consequence of their role as musicians and performers.

In his book on gypsy music, Franz Liszt described his experiences of seeing music performed in Moscow and offered

Romani musicians in 19th-century Russia.

Lyalya Chernaya Black of the Theatre Romen singing, *c.* 1960.

something of a mixed review. He found little to recommend in
the purely instrumental music, and described the opulent decor
of the venues in which the gypsy musicians performed as being
'entirely misplaced, reversed, forced and artificial'.[6] He describes
the vocal music as veering from soothing to rousing, but adds that
it had 'become largely degenerate through continual contact with
European art'. Nevertheless, he writes, 'It still retains, however,
sufficient real originality in rhythm – sufficient trace of that
furious energy which specialises it – as well as sufficient novelty
in modulation to give it an inimitable charm.'[7] Liszt's assertion
that the music became degenerate foreshadows the reasons for
the decline of the gypsy choirs. Following the Revolution in 1917,
the choirs were seen as symbols of bourgeois decadence, enjoyed
by an aristocratic elite and forming an equivalent elite from the
cadre of their performers. The romance of the gypsy was also no

longer acceptable: Roma were expected to become Soviet citizens, and that extended to the rural Roma – whom the choirs represented in some vicarious way for their audiences – as much as it did to the elite musicians. The gypsy figure represented backwardness and impenetrability in Bolshevik society, but the drive towards their assimilation was not immediate or comprehensive.[8] In the early 1920s, gypsies were regarded as a distinct group with their own identity, which needed to be supported in order for them to become fully engaged communist citizens.[9]

Further into the 1920s came a Bolshevik campaign to eliminate the gypsy choirs, but there were also those who believed that they could be incorporated into the Soviet state, most notably Nikolai Kruchinin. Ultimately, however, Kruchinin's choir was unsuccessful, being deemed closer in realization to the now unacceptable choirs than to the Soviet ideal. In 1931, the state-founded Theatre Romen was established in Moscow as a means of promoting the kind of gypsy performance that was considered acceptable at the time – the aim was that the culture it promoted was that of authentic gypsies, rather than the perceived bourgeois bastardization of the choirs. The Theatre Romen remained popular throughout the Soviet period and beyond, and continues to exist to this day.

Although it might have had an enduring cultural value, the Theatre Romen, and the Soviet state that conceived it, had a backward effect on the assimilation of Roma in Russia. Roma in Soviet Russia were required to become Soviet citizens, but also to remain identifiable as gypsies, with the state seemingly considering that the romantic elements of the gypsy could be comfortably juxtaposed with the more prosaic aspects of Soviet citizenship.[10] This in fact allowed the Roma some form of resistance. However, any such resistance required Roma to assert their gypsiness, and to reinforce the traits associated with the stereotypical gypsy figure. For example, while Romani citizens did adopt the 'Bolshevik speak' that was expected, they were also able to communicate in their own vocabularies, and could legitimately and openly do so due to their gypsy identity and the perception that they were a backward people.[11]

This might appear empowering on some levels, but it in fact put them at a disadvantage, turning them away from the assimilation that had been initiated by the choirs, and limiting their capacity to acquire social status among non-Roma. As late as the 1990s, the only career with any social status that was available to Romani people was performing with the Theatre Romen, while for those who were not singers, dancers or musicians, 'claiming relatives at the Romani Theater was one of the only forms of symbolic and social capital they could lay claim to.'[12] Ironically, this suggests that the drive to wipe out the elite created by the gypsy choirs was unsuccessful, with the Theatre Romen resulting in an elite of its own, which outlived the Soviet era. This was apparent even before the fall of the Iron Curtain. Gerald Stanton Smith wrote in 1984 that 'the gypsy theater is commonly regarded by the intelligentsia as one of the very few institutions that the Soviet state has not managed to deaden.'[13] The Theatre Romen can thus be seen as a project of limited success, which has made little difference to the performance of gypsy music in urban Russia. However, it is an interesting case study, which reveals how the fear of, and subsequent manipulation of, gypsy identity by non-Roma has the potential to result in changes in ideas of gypsy music and performance.

The Theatre Romen cannot be properly considered without being placed in the context of authenticity, which is crucial to its establishment and the way in which it was managed. Notions of the authentic were apparent and important when we discussed gypsy music from the Balkans and the way it is marketed to the West. The case of the Russian Theatre Romen is different, since

here Russian gypsy music is being sold to Russian people, and
authenticity therefore operates in a specific but no less important
manner. The distinction between urban and rural Roma is again
significant, with rural Roma being regarded as more authentic
than their urbanized counterparts, and by virtue of this their
music also being thought of as more authentic. It seems that
this was the case in the era of the choirs as much as it was after
the formation of the Theatre Romen. In 1917, the year of the
Russian Revolution, Alexander Kuprin published a sentimental
essay called 'On the Passing of the Gypsy Song in Russia',
lamenting that

> What they offer us to-day from the stage and in cabaret,
> under the alluring name of a 'gypsy-ballad', has lost its
> blood-connection with the gypsy camp, and has been
> shorn of the spirit and very essence of that strange and
> mysterious tribe.[14]

Kuprin was broadly sympathetic towards the Revolution, so it
may be the case that his essay prefigures the establishment of
the Theatre Romen.

The concern with authenticity expounded here by Kuprin
and later by the Theatre Romen is bound up with the notion
of *tsyganshchina*, which signifies an inauthentic gypsiness.
Tsyganshchina not only referred to a form of gypsy music or
performance, but also to the so-called decadence that was
associated with the bourgeois environment and social milieu
of the choirs. In order to counter this, the Theatre recruited
Roma from rural areas with the aim of putting on a more
authentic gypsy performance. However, the key performers
were in fact established members of the urban gypsy choirs,
and the rural Roma were shipped in not because they were
superior musicians or singers, but because they were thought

to contribute greater authenticity to the ensemble.[15] Alaina Lemon reveals that while undertaking fieldwork in Russia she learned that such prejudices concerning authenticity persisted for decades:

> Still, many people discouraged me from beginning research at the Romani Theater or with the Romani urban intelligentsia: they were not 'authentic'. I would not meet 'real Gypsies' if I wasted time at the Theater, declared two Russian folklorists I met briefly in early spring 1990 . . . They promised to take me to see the 'wild' (*dikije*) Gypsies of a 'real Gypsy camp' – on the condition that I read a number of nineteenth-century musicologists and bring them some batteries.[16]

In this account we see an expectation from non-Roma of how the gypsy ought to appear. Such expectations only serve to maintain the marginalization of the Romani people. Two types of Othering are at play here: those Roma who do not conform to the stereo-types associated with the gypsy figure are Othered by the standards of the gypsy figure as defined by non-Roma, while those who do conform are Othered as gypsies.

The suggestion that rural Roma are more authentic recalls the assertions of Béla Bartók, who claimed that the gypsy music played by bands in cities in Hungary was not authentic, while accepting that there was a more genuine gypsy music played by rural Roma. The example of the Theatre Romen might seem to support this argument, and this is reasonable: a style of perform-ance that is in fact a construct designed to fit in with a particular ideology seems almost fated to be inauthentic. However, Bartók's argument ultimately implied that there may be no such thing as a genuinely authentic gypsy music, so we should establish whether this is something that can also be applied in the case of Russia. By looking more closely at the style of Russian gypsy music we may be able to do so.

The instrument most closely associated with Russian gypsy music is the guitar – which is also the central instrument in the flamenco of Spain, the gypsy jazz of France and the hybridized, multinational form of gypsy punk. These styles of music have essential similarities in that they are popularly regarded as gypsy music, and in that their sound is driven by guitars, but there are considerable differences between them.

The technical feature that sets Russian guitar music apart is the type of instrument on which it is traditionally played. The guitar has seven strings, with the additional string acting as a bass, and is usually tuned to an open G major chord. This means that playing all seven strings unfretted will result in a G major chord, and other chords can be played simply by barring all the strings at the same point. However, the style of playing is typically more elaborate, with finger picking being used up and down the length of the fretboard to produce often intricate melodies and a sound that is sometimes closer to that of a lute or harp than a conventional guitar. According to Oleg Timofeyev, a Russian guitarist and academic whose doctoral thesis examined the origins of the Russian seven-string guitar, the origins of the instrument are as a hybrid: 'The shape, dimensions, and the use of gut strings were taken from the Spanish guitar, while the raised fingerboard and the chordal tuning were inherited from the English "guittar" (or some of its close relatives).'[17]

As with some of the gypsy music we have already discussed, the origins of the style do not lie with the Roma. Timofeyev considers the first half of the nineteenth century to be the 'golden age' of the seven-string guitar; he notes that during this period leading composers wrote for the Russian guitar, which also appeared in literature and art. It was only later in the nineteenth century that the seven-string guitar began to be associated with gypsies and poorer people, having fallen in esteem.[18]

Timofeyev does note that there were no doubt virtuoso players among the Roma who adopted the instrument. This recalls Liszt's interest in the virtuoso gypsy musician, and reminds us that gypsy music is generally understood with reference to its performance rather than in terms of its composition. The Russian guitar repertoire included transcriptions and variations of classical pieces, as well as original compositions. Russian composers like Mikhail Vysotsky and Andrei Sychra are credited with setting both the playing style and much of the repertoire, but Czech and Polish composers also wrote for the instrument. It was later in the nineteenth century, when the seven-string guitar became more closely associated with gypsy music, that Russian folk music was incorporated into the repertoire.[19] During the latter part of the nineteenth century and then in the twentieth, the seven-string guitar was used to accompany songs in the gypsy choirs and subsequently in the Theatre Romen.

As the twentieth century progressed, the use of the seven-string guitar, and the understanding of the gypsy song in Russia, became somewhat adapted. In his 1984 book on Russian guitar music, Stanton Smith writes:

One important type of unofficial song that has continued to exist despite occasional condemnation is the gypsy song or gypsy romance. The concept is used very vaguely in Russian to refer to songs that may have no overt reference to actual gypsies in their subject matter.[20]

In a way, this is a redundant qualification, since it is the case all over Europe that the songs played by Romani musicians, and those considered to be gypsy music, do not necessarily reference Roma, gypsies or the issues relevant to them or lifestyles associated with them. It is usually stylistic elements and the mode of performance that cause a music to be identified as gypsy

Seven-string guitar made by the California luthier Waylin Carpenter.

music, rather than lyrics and themes. However, the history of the seven-string guitar means that it has a less embedded gypsy identity than, for example, the music of the *verbunkos* tradition in Hungary. The idea of the gypsy song in Russia, therefore, is in some ways removed from the traditions of gypsy music, but also connected to them through use of the seven-string guitar and the romantic associations of the gypsy figure, which are carried over into the aura of the singer-songwriter as performer.

Stanton Smith is primarily concerned with what he describes as Russian guitar poetry, a form that emerged in the Khrushchev era, pioneered by the singer Bulat Okudzhava. The other key

Russian musician Bulat Okudzhava.

figures in the genre were Aleksandr Galich and Vladimir Vysotsky, and the heyday of the style, according to Stanton Smith, was the decade from 1962 to 1972.[21] The music was anti-establishment and often politically subversive, and recordings circulated in *magnitizdat* form – the recorded equivalent of *samizdat* literature. For Stanton Smith the use of the seven-string guitar was particularly important: he describes it as 'the most accessible of all Russian musical instruments' and suggests that its open-chord tuning makes it easy to play and creates a sound with an amateur 'aura'.[22] Indeed, the playing style of the guitar poets was typically very simple, in contrast to the elaborate playing derived from the classical tradition that characterized the instrument's sound in the nineteenth century. The guitar poets generally limited themselves to strumming and simple arpeggios, but the very particular sound of the seven-string gives a noticeable character to the music.

While there were clear practical reasons for the seven-string guitar being the instrument of choice for musicians like Okudzhava, Galich and Vysotsky, the instrument's gypsy association was also significant. Russian guitar poets were able to introduce elements of rawness, wildness and authenticity to their music simply by way of their chosen instrument, since that instrument was stereotypically associated with the gypsy figure and its representations in Russian art and music.[23] Most of their songs were short and unpolished and the singing of the guitar poets was unrefined. This is to be expected given that they came from more of a literary tradition than a musical one; their music was really little more than a backing track for their poetry. In this respect they are very different from Romani musicians, but the gypsy association has nonetheless been applied to their work.

Of course, the qualities of rawness and authenticity and their association with the gypsy figure are by no means exclusive to Russian perceptions of the gypsy. However, Russian gypsy songs and guitar poetry are of particular interest in that they reveal just how distinct from the Romani people a style of music can be whilst still being regarded in some way as gypsy music. It has also been noted that the *magnitizdat* circulation of these Russian gypsy songs means that they are wild and nomadic, thus having similarities with the romanticized gypsy figure.[24] This suggestion takes the concept of gypsy in quite a different direction, with the gypsy figure not only being associated with the music on account of the qualities it is thought to represent, but also as a metaphor for the way that the music is transmitted and consumed. Such are the pervasive stereotypes applied to the gypsy that a metaphorical reading seems perfectly valid.

Today, protest music in Russia has evolved from the singer-songwriter form to take in genres like punk and hip-hop. However, the tradition of the seven-string guitar endures as a form of folk music, and continues to have strong associations with the gypsy. The Theatre Romen in Moscow continues to perform, with the seven-string guitar still being used as a backing instrument for songs. Russian gypsy music has also been exported to the West, albeit less extensively than the gypsy music of the Balkans. The best-known groups outside Russia that use the seven-string guitar and Russian gypsy music playing style are the Kolpakov Trio and Kolpakov Duo, led by the guitarist Sasha Kolpakov. They played as part of the Gypsy Caravan tour in the USA in 2008, which sought to showcase the varied styles of music played by Romani musicians, and Vadim Kolpakov, Sasha's nephew, has also established a U.S.-based group, Via Romen.

The music of both groups is dominated by highly professional, almost virtuoso guitar playing. Sasha and Vadim Kolpakov have both previously had extensive careers playing with the Theatre Romen, and this is apparent from their polished playing style. Although there is some singing in their repertoires, it is primarily instrumental, and involves guitars playing in a polyphonic style reminiscent of string bands like Taraf de Haïdouks in the way that melodies interweave with one another. The warm timbre of the guitars contrasts with the sharper sounds of the violins and cimbaloms used in some Balkan and Hungarian music, but there are instances where the phrasing, rhythms and scales are similar. It is both guitar music and gypsy music. When the musicians play interpretations of traditional songs – the Kolpakov Duo, for example, have recorded a version of the song 'Dui Dui', which has been played by Romani musicians in Russia, Central Europe and the Balkans – it seems that they are less concerned with preserving the songs in an authentic form than with asserting their own place in the contemporary canon of Romani musicians. Although the lineage to early Russian guitar composers like Vysotsky and Sychra is apparent – and the Kolpakovs have collaborated with Oleg Timofeyev on an album of early Russian gypsy music – the tradition in which they play is very much that of folk and gypsy music rather than classical.

The relative obscurity of this style of music, compared to bands like Taraf de Haïdouks and Fanfare Ciocărlia, is a sign of how important record labels and their marketing are to the contemporary understanding of gypsy music in the West. Labels like Crammed Discs and Asphalt Tango have established legends around the musicians they promote and achieved considerable success. However, Opre Records, the Swiss label that released the Kolpakov Trio's album *Rodava Tut* (1995), their only record marketed in Western Europe, seem far less concerned with commercializing the music, and more interested in preserving the sound of Romani music (their only other release, *Pilem Pilem* by the Austrian-based Serbian Romani group Rromano Centar, who play the stringed instruments of the tamburica family, is similarly obscure). Accordingly, the wider sense of what constitutes gypsy music today is informed only by those traditions and sounds that have been more aggressively promoted by record labels.

Although Russian gypsy music is less well known in the West than its Balkan counterparts, there is an association between Russia and the gypsy figure that extends to gypsy music. This is in part a result of the music itself, particularly that of the gypsy choirs and the Theatre Romen. While these styles of gypsy music are not particularly popular in the West, there is a tacit connection between Russia and Eastern Europe in the Western imagination, which means that on some level the two regions are conflated and Russian gypsy music is seen as being of a piece with Balkan gypsy music. Accordingly, Russian gypsy music, which shares some rhythms and accents with the gypsy music of the Balkans, may sound to Western ears like Balkan gypsy music, and thus inform an association between Russia and the gypsies. Similarly, the contiguities of these gypsy musics might also inform an association between Russia and the Balkans.

Of course, this association is embedded more deeply in Russian history. We have already seen how Pushkin's poem 'The Gypsies' presented a highly romanticized image of Romani culture and implied that it was straightforward for non-Roma to become gypsy. This is in fact just one instance of a fascination with the gypsy figure that is quite prevalent in Russian literature, to the point that the gypsy can be seen almost as a symbol of Russia. Lemon describes how the gypsy figure has become an 'emblem of the nation' in that it evokes the poets who portrayed and defined it, including Pushkin, Fet, Grigoriev and Gorky.[25] This is also the case with gypsy musicians, who have been portrayed in music, literature and theatre in order to introduce rawness and authenticity.[26] David Malvinni, meanwhile, argues that some of the work of Rachmaninov may have been influenced by gypsy music, indicating that Romani culture also seeped into the classical tradition in Russia in a similar way to what happened in Hungary.[27] Like some of Liszt's piano pieces, a number of Rachmaninov's are noted for their difficulty, and he also composed two rhapsodies, so there is a case for placing him in a tradition of classical music being informed by gypsy music.

We have already discerned that there is an association between gypsy music and the Balkans, which exists due to similarities in perception that affect both the Roma and the Balkan region. Following on from this, it is possible to hypothesize that there may be a similar tie between gypsy music and Russia. Certainly, there are similarities in the Western popular imagination in how Russia and the Balkans are perceived. If we work through the characteristics that we previously established as being commonly applied to the Balkans this will become clear.

The first characteristic is that the Balkans are thought of as being not quite part of, yet not quite outside of, Europe. This can also be applied to Russia, which, in its huge size, straddles the continents of Europe and Asia, and includes the cities of Moscow and St Petersburg in the west, significant cities in a European tradition, and more exoticized, remote locations such as Siberia and Sakhalin in the east. Secondly, we considered the uncertain political geography of the Balkans, which has been prone to change and which has led to confusion about borders. Again, there are similarities in the case of Russia, most significantly the period following the break-up of the USSR, which resulted in several often-confused countries reasserting their national identities in central Asia.

Our final point was the perception that the Balkans are war-torn and corrupt. While there is less popular perception of Russia as a war-torn country, its association with corruption is even more pronounced than is the case with the Balkans; and, as we saw when we addressed perceptions of the Balkans, this has much to do with the notion of the Soviet legacy. The sense of corruption and dishonesty that was tied to the communist era has clung on in the Western imagination, and in the case of Russia this is arguably more pronounced than in the Balkans due to the ongoing corruption that is widely understood to be underpinning Vladimir Putin's current regime. This association with corruption is also frequently applied to the Romani people: accordingly we can begin to see that certain countries are regarded within the framework of the same stereotypes as are attached to the Roma. It is perhaps too great a leap to suggest that the countries in question are always those with significant Romani populations – similar stereotypes of corruption are also applied to Asian and African countries that do not have significant numbers of Roma. However, examining the prevalence of stereotypes in certain countries alongside the Roma and their music might help us to draw more useful connections and conclusions.

Having begun to consider the sound, history and reception of gypsy music from locations outside the Balkans, we can start to establish parallels and differences. Clearly, the guitar- and vocal-driven gypsy music of Russia is quite different in its style and sound from the gypsy musics of the Balkans – which, as we know, are in themselves very diverse. The specific sound of Russian gypsy music can be accounted for at least in part by the historic context in which it was performed in gypsy choirs and in the Theatre Romen. Additionally, it has been less affected than the Balkans by efforts to market the music outside of Russia: whereas Balkan gypsy music has continued to change in order to meet the commercial expectations of Western record labels, Russian gypsy music has arguably evolved more slowly, and the sound of the seven-string guitar has remained an enduring one.

On the other hand, there are parallels in the exoticization of the Roma that takes place through gypsy music consumption by non-Roma, and which is a constant in both the Balkans and in Russia, as well as among audiences elsewhere who listen to the music. In both cases there is also a demand for what is perceived as authenticity, and this is bound up in a distinction made between urban and rural settings – in both Russia and in the Balkans it is presumed that the more authentic gypsy music will derive from rural areas, even though there is nothing intrinsically more authentic about this music, and although the standard of musicianship may in fact be lower. Finally, it is clear from the case of Russia that something similar to balkanism – something between balkanism and Orientalism – can be applied to certain countries outside of the Balkans, and that this is illuminated when examined in the context of a country's Romani population.

6 GYPSY MUSIC IN SPAIN: FLAMENCO

Earlier, we touched upon the films of Emir Kusturica; with their gypsy music soundtracks and portrayals of romanticized gypsies they present the Balkans and the Roma who live there in a way that conforms to the stereotypes of the West. There is perhaps an alternative representation to be found in the work of Tony Gatlif, a French film-maker who is of Romani descent. He has been making films that engage with the Roma since the early 1980s, but his breakthrough came in 1993 with *Latcho Drom*, whose title can be literally translated from the Romani as 'safe journey'.

Although this film is presented as a documentary, it is in fact entirely staged. Its subject-matter is the historic journey from Rajasthan made by Romani people over several centuries, and the device that Gatlif uses to chronicle the diaspora is music. Thus, *Latcho Drom* begins with an episode that shows the traditional music of the contemporary inhabitants of Rajasthan, before moving west through Turkey, Egypt and Eastern Europe and into France and Spain, where it concludes with a performance by the flamenco singer La Caita. As with the Gypsy Caravan tour, the diversity of the styles that have been placed within the remit of gypsy music is emphasized, and the commonalities and differences that these forms have are revealed.

Flamenco is widely considered to be a gypsy style. It has antecedents in Arabic and Moorish music and culture along with that of the Roma, and has come to be a signifier of Spain

Café Cantante, Spain, *c.* 1888.

as well as of the gypsy figure, but its gypsiness is central both to its history and its perception. There has, however, been critical debate about how central the Roma are to flamenco. Although Arabic, Indian, Jewish and Byzantine influences are acknowledged, the Roma are generally seen as crucial, and Romani musicians remain prevalent in the contemporary flamenco scene.[1] However, there is sometimes a tendency to romanticize about gypsies when discussing the history and performance of flamenco.[2] It is important to note that while some flamenco musicians do not claim any particular ethnic identity, others do identify as gypsy or *gitano*.[3]

We will come back to the figure of the *gitano*, and the question of what that figure represents, in due course; for now let us focus on the sound and history of flamenco. There are four key elements in flamenco: singing, dance, guitar playing and *jaleo*, the articulation of vocal accents.[4] Its repertoire is defined less by particular songs then by styles, such as lively tangos and fandangos, and soulful seguirillas, which are improvised around by singers and musicians. Flamenco is more than simply a form of music; in addition to the other art forms that are involved in its performance, it is also regarded by some performers and commentators as a philosophy.[5] But it is the music that we will focus on here, and the importance of guitar playing and singing to its sound means that connections might be made between flamenco and the Russian gypsy music that we have already examined – which add fuel to the argument that flamenco is very much a gypsy music.

The flamenco style of guitar playing is more sophisticated than Russian gypsy guitar, however, and we can draw comparisons with the virtuosity associated with gypsy music from the Balkans and Hungary. The guitar used is also different, and has evolved to suit the style of playing; its thin body and light weight ensure that the strings do not sustain too long and that the rapid sequences of notes can be heard as a sequence rather than as a blur. If flamenco were played on the seven-string guitar favoured by the Russian guitar poets, the sound would be muddied.

D. E. Pohren groups flamenco into four categories – deep, intermediate, light and popular – which he presents as if ranked in order of importance and artistic value. At the bottom of this hierarchy is the popular flamenco that is played largely for the benefit of tourists, while at the top is deep flamenco, which Pohren describes as 'the means by which a manic-depressive society expresses its black moods'.[6] This is a striking description, which demonstrates Pohren's own romanticization of Romani lifestyles and music, but it also reveals evidence of further stereotyping. Firstly, there is the obvious association between gypsy music and depression, characterizing the Roma as a melancholy and desperate people who can only be cured through playing music. Additionally, and as is the case with so much of the gypsy music we have seen, it places value on authenticity.

Deep flamenco music, known as *canto jondo*, is presented as a direct line of contact to the dark soul of the gypsy, and it is for this reason that it is described as more valuable than the lighter forms of the genre. In deep flamenco the guitar is less important; the singer is the focal point and in some cases songs are performed without accompaniment. In contrast, in more popular flamenco the guitar is often played as a solo instrument; this is a marked departure from the vocal-led tradition of deep song.

These distinctions, or hierarchies, between types of flamenco connect with discourses of authenticity that exist more broadly in gypsy music and world music, but in addition are connected to a more general dichotomy within the genre: flamenco is seen as being simultaneously a folk music and a professional music. On one hand it is thought of as being a form that is thoroughly demotic; on the other it is placed on the same stages and viewed through the same critical lenses as classical music. As Timothy Mitchell puts it:

> Perhaps the biggest paradox of all is that flamenco is a style of folk music that reached such heights of elaboration that its full enjoyment and appreciation came to be monopolized not by the folk but by a discerning elite of Spanish playboys and connoisseurs.[7]

This is by no means a paradox that is unique to flamenco. Clearly it is also the case with Russian gypsy music, which has been perceived as a style directly connected to rural encampments, but which evolved into a form that was condemned by Bolsheviks as being a pleasure of the bourgeoisie. We can also find this dichotomy of folk and professionalism in Balkan gypsy music. Although commentators such as Liszt and George Borrow have presented the gypsy as a simple figure able to express himself in music only by some kind of fluke, the virtuosity which is evident in the music of the Roma means that it is also connected with a more formal, classical tradition. Considering gypsy music in terms of the spaces of its performance highlights the contrast further. Gypsy music might be associated in the popular imagination with campfires, caravans and itinerancy, but the gypsy music exported to the West is often played in huge concert halls. In London, for example, gypsy music concerts have been held in rock and pop music venues, but also formal, seated theatres such as the Royal Festival Hall and the Barbican Theatre. Evidently, this dichotomy between folk and professional music can be mapped onto the dichotomy between rural and urban gypsy music performance that we have already identified.

Pohren connects the professionalization and commercialization of flamenco with a decline in the form that he identifies as beginning in the early twentieth century, following a nineteenth-century golden age.[8] However, he credits the subsequent interest in flamenco from foreigners with bringing about a revival.[9] This is significant when taken in the context of authenticity, which as we have seen is so important to gypsy music in all its guises. Given that Pohren has already ranked flamenco according to a hierarchy based on artistic value, a subtext of authenticity can be read into his comments about its decline: it is as though flamenco declined in its authenticity. Interestingly, Pohren suggests that it was revived by interest from outside Spain: this might indicate that consumers of gypsy music from outside of its immediate culture have a greater stake in determining whether or not a particular mode of gypsy music should be deemed to be authentic.

The Balkan examples of Taraf de Haïdouks and Fanfare Ciocărlia support this hypothesis. The marketing of these groups in the West makes much of the fact that they are from rural villages in Romania, as if this should mean that they are closer to a sense of tradition and authenticity – yet their music has to be taken out of these settings and into the concert halls of Western Europe and the United States before such judgements and pronouncements of authenticity can be made.

For flamenco, the archetypal authentic setting of the style is Andalusia in southern Spain, where it is regarded as having its origins as a form that is culturally hybrid. Although flamenco is thought of as a gypsy, or *gitano*, music, it is also thought of as being distinctly Andalusian in character, and this is particularly the case within Spain. This is, however, a more recent phenomenon: during the years of the Franco dictatorship, flamenco was appropriated as a symbol of national identity in Spain, but latterly it has been reclaimed as a regional form and symbol in Andalusia.[10]

This Andalusian regionalism might have parallels with an imagined gypsy regionalism, which can be identified not only within flamenco, but also in other kinds of gypsy music outside Spain. In addition, the Roma have been adopted as part of the Andalusian regionalism of flamenco. It is right that this should be the case, since it is universally acknowledged that Roma in Spain were instrumental in the development of flamenco – but in some commentaries there is a sense that the contribution of the Roma to flamenco's sound has been to introduce elements of foreignness or Otherness.[11] It has also been suggested that Roma are responsible for the origins of flamenco, and their contribution is defined in terms of their musicality; the stereotyping, romanticization and Othering of the Roma is enacted in the context of flamenco in the same way that it is in the contexts of other forms of gypsy music.[12]

In 2010, flamenco was inscribed on UNESCO's List of the Intangible Cultural Heritage of Humanity. Although UNESCO's description of flamenco does not directly define it as a gypsy music, it is described as 'the badge of identity of numerous communities and groups, in particular the Gitano (Roma) ethnic community, which has played an essential role in its development'.[13] The presence of flamenco on the UNESCO list should not be seen as an effort to preserve an idea of gypsy music or the musical culture of the Roma – no other style of music that might be considered gypsy is included on the list – but perhaps this is not a serious failing.

While it is undoubtedly important that the musical culture of the Roma is recognized, we know that it is a musical culture that is informed substantially by the ways in which Romani musicians have interacted with non-Roma, responding to local folk music traditions in the areas where they have travelled and settled, and performing for non-Romani audiences. In the case of flamenco, a hybridity can be identified which on one hand might seem to define it as less of a gypsy music. But this sense of hybridity is evidently crucial to many kinds of gypsy music, and thus it is valid to describe flamenco as a form of gypsy music.

While it is certainly reasonable to consider flamenco a gypsy music, it should not be forgotten that it is at the same time a form of music indigenous to Spain. It is therefore important to consider the history of the Roma in Spain, and the way that the gypsy figure has been perceived specifically in the Spanish context, if we wish to fully understand flamenco as a gypsy music.

It seems likely that Roma first arrived in Spain in the early fifteenth century. George Borrow gives this date in his book on Roma in Spain, and 1425 has been cited elsewhere as the date when the Roma began to cross the Pyrenees and arrive in Spain, while those who arrived later in the fifteenth century claimed to have travelled from Greece.[14] It is likely that the Roma were playing music in Spain on a professional level as soon as they arrived, and therefore that there was gypsy music in Spain before flamenco was established.[15] This is certainly plausible, if Romani people did indeed travel from Greece or the Balkans, where they were already active as musicians; and it supports the consensus that flamenco emerged as a style that was developed by Roma, Andalusians and perhaps other groups.

There had not been a Romani presence in Spain for long before laws began to be passed that discriminated against them and their lifestyles – just as was the case in the Balkans. The first anti-gypsy laws were passed in 1499, with Roma being required to settle and take up trades, or to become servants. More laws were passed during the sixteenth century onwards with the aim of bringing about forced assimilation – in the early seventeenth century, for example, the word *gitano* was banned – but they began to be relaxed towards the end of the eighteenth century.[16] It is ironic that this kind of institutionalized discrimination was going on even as the Roma were filling in gaps in the economy that had been left open due to previous xenophobic and discriminatory practices. Andalusia had the largest and most integrated Romani population in Spain, and this was a result of Roma taking on economic roles that had previously been occupied by the recently expelled Moorish population.[17] Without this level of integration in Andalusia it seems unlikely that flamenco would have developed in the way that it did.

Roma in Spain have also been subject to widespread stereotyping and exoticization, as they have all over Europe. Pohren's book on flamenco is guilty of perpetuating this. Just as he divides flamenco into categories of authenticity, he splits Spanish Roma into three types: those who have entered into *payo*, or non-Romani life, those on the fringes of the non-Romani community, and those who 'have remained true to their trad-itional way of life, and have thus far rejected *payo* society'.[18] Displaying a romanticizing attitude and a striving towards perceived authenticity in Romani culture, he goes on to set out a kind of hierarchy in which the nomadic Roma of Spain are seen as, and see themselves as, superior to those who have settled into *payo* society.[19]

This viewpoint is very much in line with much writing on the gypsy figure, but in the Spanish context it is necessary to address the more specific figure of the *gitano*. It is arguable that entrenched perceptions mean that there is in fact little difference between the *gitano* and the gypsy, but some commentators have used *gitano* not as another word for Roma or gypsy, but to denote a wider group, arguing that escaped slaves, Moorish peasants, Jews and all manner of outcasts also attached themselves to groups of Romani *gitanos* and became assimilated with them.[20]

But this can also be read as an interpretation of the state of gypsiness being defined by lifestyle rather than race or inheritance. These *gitanos* are more like the gypsies of stereotypes and stories than the Romani people; the *gitano* understood in this way is essentially no different from the gypsies that can be found in the novels of George Borrow and the ethnographies of writers like Judith Okely.[21] Once again, this is gypsiness as an adopted rather than a racially inscribed characteristic. Flamenco has been described as an identity symbol that some *gitanos* have chosen to make use of, the implication being that the *gitanos* who play flamenco will present themselves as living up to the gypsy stereotypes expected of them by their audience.[22] Flamenco might be an identity symbol, and something that some *gitanos* use to identify themselves; however, it is also a stereotype that is often applied to Roma by non-Roma, so it is not without complications.

Gitanismo, a specific romanticization of the *gitano*, which has obvious parallels with the more general romanticization of the gypsy figure more widely in Europe, pervades flamenco. Themes of freedom, persecution and gypsy lore can be found in flamenco lyrics, raising the question of whether gypsy identity is defined from within or without the actual culture of the Roma.[23]

Gitanismo, along with the interest in authentic flamenco that is wrapped up within it, arguably has more directly negative consequences for the Roma. Supposedly interethnic flamenco events do not necessarily bring Roma and non-Roma any closer together, and there have been instances of Romani performers being exploited by tour operators who perpetuate stereotypes while making commercial gain from *gitano* performance.[24]

A more complex relationship between Roma and non-Roma, and one that is also closely connected to flamenco, can be found in the work of the poet Federico García Lorca, whose poetry frequently uses themes from flamenco and the idea of the *gitano*. Lorca is credited with developing the notion of *duende*, a heightened sense of soul or spirit, which is applicable to many forms of art and music, but which is often identified – by Lorca among many others – as a characteristic of flamenco.[25] In his defining lecture on *duende*, Lorca associates this feeling with death and darkness in a kind of Othering of the concept – an Othering that mirrors the way the Roma have been Othered for centuries.

Flamenco was also an important influence on Lorca's poetry, not only in thematic terms, but also in terms of form; indeed, the brief, almost fragmentary form of flamenco lyrics, in which the poetry of the verses is more important than any sense of narrative, was influential on the wider development of short poems in the Spanish language. Lorca trained as a musician before he began to write poetry, and along with his friend the composer Manuel de Falla, who was also influenced by flamenco, he organized the first amateur festival of deep flamenco in 1921.[26] It was around this time that he wrote his *Poem of the Deep Song*, in which flamenco and the motif of the guitar recur often. Although there are a number of *gitano* references in his subsequent collection *The Gypsy Ballads* (1928), these poems are less concerned with the gypsy or *gitano* figure than the title might suggest; rather they evoke a mood of tradition, romance and strife that can be loosely

Federico García Lorca.

related to the stereotypical gypsy figure. Indeed, the title of *The Gypsy Ballads* might be equated with the Russian gypsy songs of the twentieth century that we previously encountered, insofar as they suggest that a poem can be presented as gypsy without directly referencing the Roma or gypsiness.

Lorca's portrayals of flamenco and the *gitano* figure are perhaps summed up by Peter Manuel's comment on flamenco and the popular imagination: 'The widespread traditional misconception of Gypsies as merry and carefree hedonists has been one unfortunate product of the popular misunderstanding of flamenco.'[27] Manuel also acknowledges the use of flamenco by Franco's regime to present a more idyllic image of Spain, both for those inside and outside the country. But this perception of Spain from outside, which has clear parallels with non-Romani perceptions of the gypsy, is in fact something that existed well before Franco.

Earlier, we discussed the examples of Cervantes's *La Gitanilla* and Prosper Mérimée's novella *Carmen* in the context of their portrayals of the gypsy figure. However, it is significant that these texts specifically portray gypsies in Spain. In the introduction to his 2004 translation of *Carmen*, Andrew Brown suggests that it might be

> more a work of cultural anthropology than a love story. It is, after all, shot through with the 'otherness' that is the main object of all anthropological study. A Frenchman is writing a story about Spain – or rather about two Spaniards who are not entirely Spanish (whatever that might mean): don José, who is a Basque, and Carmen who is a Gypsy.[28]

As Brown intimates, *Carmen* is as much about Spain as an Other as it is about gypsies as Others. Indeed, Mérimée's novella involves what has been described as 'the conflation of Gypsy, Andalusian, and Spanish identities as mutually interchangeable signifiers'.[29] This sense of conflation only became more pronounced when *Carmen* was adapted into an opera by Georges Bizet, first performed in 1875, at a time when enthusiasm for the gypsy figure remained strong across Europe.

Spain was also perceived through an exoticizing gaze, seen as being more oriental than other European countries, and the gypsy has been seen as one facet of that identity.[30] This is arguably even more applicable to Andalusia, the Spanish region most closely associated with flamenco and the *gitano* figure. Borrow is prone to such Orientalism of Andalusia, and connects the native population of the region with the *gitanos*: 'The Andalusians are a mixed breed of various nations, Romans, Vandals, Moors; perhaps there is a slight sprinkling of Gypsy blood in their veins, and of Gypsy fashion in their garb.'[31] This connection is also made by Bernard Leblon, who rightly ascribes the origins of flamenco to a Romani-Andalusian hybrid, but who also attributes this hybrid in part to the shared traits he claims to identify in the two groups.[32] This is of course unhelpful, being likely to result in the perpetuation of stereotypes about both groups, and shedding little more light on the roots of flamenco.

The notion of an oriental Spain is particularly interesting in the wider context of gypsy music. Earlier, we considered the idea of balkanism, which has a clear precedent in Orientalism.[33] Accordingly, we might be able to propose that something similar and related to both balkanism and Orientalism could be applied to Spain. In considering perceptions of Russia from outside, and how such perceptions can be mapped on to the representation of Roma in Russia, we established that there are tacit links between Russia and Eastern Europe in the Western popular imagination.

In the case of Spain we cannot make such links, nor can we apply the characteristics we have identified as defining perceptions of the Balkans. The geography of Spain is quite clear to those from outside Spain; its status as a European country is not open to question; it is no more the butt of jokes than is any other Western European country; and there is little sense of corruption. Some affinities with the communist regime can be found in the Franco dictatorship, which to some extent defined Spain for much of the twentieth century, but Franco's authoritarianism did not correlate in the popular imagination with the blight associated with communist regimes further east, and is less easily connected with the gypsy figure.

However, the profound Otherness bound up in Orientalism clearly does give Spain links with the figure of the gypsy. Spain has been described as having experienced Orientalism both as a Western European Christian culture that Orientalizes other regions and people – overlooking some of its own antecedents as it does so – and also as a part of Western Europe that is seen from outside as more Oriental.[34] Spain's status within Europe, and that of the Roma within Spain, has been defined according to an 'internal alterity'.[35] Indeed, this sense of internal alterity could be applied to Roma in many other countries, including Russia and any number of Balkan countries.

The notion of the white gypsy, a mixed-race figure portrayed in twentieth-century Spanish cinema, might help to explain this. In being both white and gypsy, this figure was an emblem of Otherness, but 'kept this excess at the margin so as to retain the fantasy that society's main antagonism was to be found at this margin, within itself'.[36] This could be applied to portrayals of the Roma much more widely, particularly within gypsy music. For example, the gypsy music of the Balkans, which as we have already described is marketed for specifically Western audiences, must have a distinct sense of difference or Otherness, but requires the Western audience to claim some form of affinity with the gypsy performer – hence the 'margin' is essential. This is the case in Balkan music exported to the West, Russian gypsy music played in the Theatre Romen, and in flamenco played for Spanish non-Roma and tourists alike.

Spanish flamenco musicians like the singer Camarón de la Isla and the guitarist Paco de Lucía became extremely popular in Spain in the 1970s and '80s, but there is a slightly unexpected coda to the relationship between flamenco and the *gitano* figure in Spain in the international success of the Gipsy Kings, a group that has garnered a huge level of global popularity for its flamenco pop music. What is unexpected is that the Gipsy Kings are in fact from France: it is rather ironic that one of the most famous bands associated with flamenco is not Andalusian or even Spanish. However, they are not completely dissociated from Spain: founding members Nicolas and André Reyes are the sons of flamenco artist Jose Reyes and were brought up in a Romani family that had migrated from Spain during the Spanish Civil War. The fact that a popular flamenco band does not need to be from Spain is of course a consequence of the highly globalized world in which we now live; widespread immigration and the easier transmission of musical styles between countries and even continents means that it is less straightforward to read specific places in sounds.

We know that certain sounds continue to be associated with specific places, and certain sounds continue to be associated with the figure of the gypsy. Yet increasingly there is a blurring of these associations and this becomes more prominent in the forms of gypsy music that have developed within the past hundred years, such as gypsy jazz, gypsy punk and Balkan beats.

7 GYPSY JAZZ: HYBRID FORMS

Comparable in its sound to flamenco, but very different in its origins, is gypsy jazz. Both flamenco and gypsy jazz can be described as hybrid forms of music, which involve gypsy music elements alongside other distinctive sounds, but there are significant differences in how their hybridization occurred. As we have established, flamenco is the product of different ethnic groups, primarily Roma and Andalusians, coming together musically. The origin of gypsy jazz, on the other hand, can be traced and credited to a single musician.

The man universally acknowledged as the founder and forefather of gypsy jazz is the guitarist Jean Reinhardt – better known as Django – who was born in 1910 in Belgium into a Romani family. The name gypsy jazz might be the product of its founding musician's ethnicity as much as the result of its sound, but the gypsy music that Reinhardt had known from his childhood was undoubtedly influential on the music he would go on to play. 'Throughout his childhood, Django was surrounded by music . . . For the Manouches and Gitans, music was as intrinsic to life as air,' his biographer, Michael Dregni, writes.[1] This may reduce Reinhardt to a stereotypical gypsy musician, but the interest in music that gripped him from an early age is irrefutable.

Reinhardt's Romani background is one of two key factors that informed both the sound of gypsy jazz and the mythology that has come to surround it. The other is the fire that engulfed his caravan when he was eighteen years old, and which badly injured the fourth and fifth fingers of his left hand. Having grown up a promising guitarist, he was forced to adapt his style of playing dramatically, forming unique chord shapes that informed the sound of gypsy jazz. Prior to his injury he played in dance halls, known as *bals-musettes*, where the music performed was regarded as what Benjamin Givan describes as 'the site of an authentically Gallic culture, relatively free of the American influences that permeated much French visual art and classical music at the time'.[2]

Here, as with *verbunkos* in Hungary, brass band music in the Balkans and flamenco in Spain, we find another example of Romani musicians playing music that has strong national associations, and further evidence that what is regarded as gypsy music continues to be informed by the musical cultures that prevail where Roma settle. However, while playing in Paris in his late teens, Reinhardt was introduced to jazz and, taken with this American import, he began to revise his playing style further. It is arguable that he had an affinity with jazz because of the weight it places on improvisation: the use of improvisation is something that gypsy music and jazz arguably have in common, as we will go on to consider.[3]

Within his lifetime, Reinhardt was best known for playing with the Quintette du Hot Club de France, in which he was one of two key members, along with violinist Stéphane Grappelli. The peak of his career was the 1930s and '40s, but at this point gypsy jazz had not been identified as a distinct genre or style; Reinhardt was understood to be both a jazz musician and a gypsy, but these two identities had not yet been conflated into a particular form of music.[4] Indeed, it was not until the 1970s, some years after Reinhardt's death from a brain haemorrhage in 1953, that the style was first termed *jazz tzigane* by gypsy jazz guitarist Francis-Alfred Moerman.

Django Reinhardt, *c.* 1946.

The Quintette du Hot Club de France was atypical among jazz bands in that it consisted solely of string instruments: Reinhardt's lead guitar and Grappelli's violin were backed by two rhythm guitars and a bass. This line-up contributed to the distinctive gypsy jazz sound. As with flamenco the guitar tone is bright and percussive, although with chords and scales derived from jazz, and the violin provides a counterpoint to the guitar melodies, introducing a smoother contrast to the staccato guitar sounds. The string band format means that a link can be made to the tradition of string bands in the Balkans and their contemporary descendants like Taraf de Haïdouks, and the rhythm guitars of gypsy jazz display a similar bounce to the cimbalom. This may be one reason beside Reinhardt's Romani ethnicity that explains why the gypsy label has continued to cling to his music.

Reinhardt has left a significant legacy, with gypsy jazz enduringly popular around the world, both in a form close to its original sound and in fusions that blend it with other styles of jazz and folk. The extent to which it is considered a gypsy music is variable: generally the gypsy jazz scene is closer to the wider jazz scene than to popular manifestations of gypsy music such as the Gypsy Caravan tour. However, while gypsy jazz has a global appeal, it is still played by Romani musicians in Western Europe, with French guitarist Biréli Lagrène being among the best known, and therefore remains both a gypsy music and a Romani music.[5]

With his best-known compositions, Reinhardt formed something of a gypsy jazz canon entirely by himself. Pieces like 'Minor Swing' and 'Nuages' have been featured on countless compilations and continue to be played by gypsy jazz musicians. Both have become archetypal gypsy jazz songs, 'Minor Swing' known for its bouncing rhythm and lilting melodies, while 'Nuages' is slower and more keening with Grappelli's violin more prominent. Even Lagrène, who is highly regarded in his own right, has included recordings of both songs, amongst many more of Reinhardt's, on several of his albums. Countless contemporary gypsy jazz groups mark themselves out as performers in their chosen genre by including the words 'Hot Club' in their names, another indication of the strength of Reinhardt's legacy.

The Reinhardt oeuvre also contains some examples of Romani songs. His song 'Tears' is a slow-paced swing piece, which is in fact based on a Romani lullaby called 'Muri Wachsella an u Sennelo Weesch' (Blackberries Grow in the Green Woods). Dregni describes it as 'unique in jazz – a Gypsy song harmonized with jazzy diminished, minor sixth, and minor seventh chords, casting a dark mood, bittersweet and melancholy'.[6] Another example cited by Dregni is 'Les Yeux Noirs', the B-side of the more famous 'Nuages', recorded under the Nazi occupation of France. 'Whether Django meant the song as a protest against the Nazi war on the Romani or not,' writes Dregni, 'it was without doubt a powerful jazz statement of Gypsy identity and pride.'[7] 'Les Yeux Noirs' is in fact a Russian song; if Reinhardt saw it as a piece of gypsy music when he recorded his version of it then this is testament to the ways in which gypsy music travels between cultures and countries.

The notion of authenticity – perennially important in the context of gypsy music, as we know – is also significant in the context of jazz, and thus carries over into gypsy jazz from two sides. The jazz critic Hugues Panassié, who vehemently argued that jazz is an intrinsically black music and who was highly critical of most non-black jazz musicians, made a rare exception in the case of Reinhardt and gypsy jazz:

It is interesting to note that Django, one of the rare white musicians comparable to the Negroes, belongs to a race which has remained very primitive, for in truth the Gypsies' lives and customs are closer to those of the Negroes than those of the whites.[8]

This passage is cited by Andy Fry in his book on African American music in France, where he notes, 'In this interpretation, then, it was not Reinhardt's French civilization but precisely his lack of it that warranted celebration.'[9] Panassié's point is clearly problematic, but it is revealing in what it says about perceptions of Romani culture and music. The suggestion that more primitive cultures might be more skilled with music recalls both the Theatre Romen in Russia bringing in rural Roma to play in urban ensembles, and Liszt's assertion that the Roma were only capable of expressing themselves via music.

Along with authenticity, romanticization is another key issue that we have had to address in the context of gypsy music, and this too has affected gypsy jazz. One particular area where it has been directed is the injury sustained by Django Reinhardt in the famous fire that necessitated his change in playing style. It is not difficult to see why this has been the case: the fact that Reinhardt was able to overcome this adversity, retaining his musical aptitude and pioneering a new style, is of course a highly appealing story, and would remain so whatever his ethnicity. However, the degree to which Reinhardt's injury affected his playing has been questioned, as there is some debate as to how much function he had in the fingers of his left hand.[10] Reinhardt's achievement in surmounting his injury may have been substantial, but while it has become a significant part of the legends that grew around him, it was evidently not a great hindrance to him.[11]

Indeed, there is no particular reason why Reinhardt's injury should be the subject of great interest, romanticization or myth-ologization, since his talent was such that his disability had no adverse affect on his playing. This unwarranted romanticization might be equated to the manner in which the Roma have been romanticized. The gypsy figure, having long been associated with criminality, dirtiness and primitiveness, can be thought of as being in some way injured in the popular imagination, since injury and disability constitute a further form of Otherness. This is a long-standing perception: indeed, in his description of the Roma he encountered, Liszt deploys a noble savage discourse, suggesting that they are not sufficiently intelligent to possess any great malice.[12] In fact, if the Roma are thought of as being injured, then it would be more correct to say that they have suffered injuries of a kind as a consequence of the negative perceptions and persistent persecution that has dogged them for centuries.

The case of Reinhardt's injury is another indicator that consumers of music – and perhaps consumers of gypsy music in particular – thrive on romanticization. It is difficult to speculate on how his musical career would have played out had he not had to overcome his injury, and it is similarly challenging to speculate on how far his injury informed his success – although it seems unreasonable to posit that he would not have pioneered gypsy jazz had his fingers still been able to make conventional chord shapes. However, the fact that he was a Rom – and specifically, a Rom who played jazz – was clearly important. The long-standing association between the gypsy and music was taken in a new direction by Reinhardt, and it was received both as a gypsy music and as an original and exciting new style.

Despite Reinhardt's enduring renown, gaps in his biography remain, and biographers have sometimes filled these gaps with anecdotes. Anecdote has thus been a constant in narratives of his life, just as it has been considered a constant point of reference in jazz.[13] Anecdote is important to the discourse of jazz as a genre operating within an oral tradition and has provided a form of empowerment for jazz musicians, providing an alternative form of response to critical discourses on jazz from outside.[14] Gypsy music is likewise attached to an oral tradition. In both forms, musicians rarely read sheet music, and improvisation is important – though it is far more important in jazz. Accordingly, one might posit that anecdote is similarly important to gypsy music, and that as with the jazz anecdote it can act as a means of empowerment.

But while jazz can also be compared to gypsy music in terms of its cultural and racial contexts, having originated with African Americans who were experiencing prejudice and discrimination comparable to that experienced by Romani people, the jazz musician's capacity for empowerment through use of anecdote is arguably greater than that of the Romani musician. The reasons for this are various. Firstly, while there is still much progress to be made, black Americans have, in general, reached a point of greater empowerment than Romani people in Europe; therefore black jazz musicians are already in a stronger position than Romani musicians who play gypsy music and their voices are less likely to be suppressed. Secondly, jazz has been written about more widely than gypsy music, and there is a greater range of criticism for jazz anecdote to respond to than is the case with gypsy music.

Finally, although many distinct styles have developed within American jazz music, it is a newer and more unified form; most musicians working within the genre are playing within a similar framework, and can communicate in the same language. Romani musicians, on the other hand, play a range of styles, some of them centuries old, which do not necessarily interrelate particularly easily, and although some commentators talk of an implicit sense of Romani unity that transcends other cultural and linguistic barriers, Roma from different countries do not always have a common language.

However, it is worth noting that due to the diversity amongst Romani musicians and styles of gypsy music, different possibilities of empowerment may apply to different musicians. Django Reinhardt, for instance, has largely avoided the negative perceptions associated with the Roma. This is to some extent equally true of many other performers of gypsy music, since the romanticized discourse of music tends to override the pejorative discourse so often applied to the Roma, but in Reinhardt's case I would argue that it is more pronounced. This is partly due to the kind of music he was famous for – as a clearly hybrid form, gypsy jazz is received and regarded somewhat differently to other forms of gypsy music, with the complex figure of the gypsy being less immediately linked to it. Additionally, the fact that Reinhardt was born in and lived in Western Europe gave him greater possibilities for empowerment than Eastern European Roma who are seen through the overlapping lenses of anti-Romani sentiment and balkanism.

Yet forms of gypsy music that have come about in Western Europe have also been subjected to romanticization and have been invoked in accounts which perpetuate problematic stereotypes. A striking set of parallels can be found in accounts of Romani life in two books about gypsy music in Western Europe: D. E. Pohren's book on flamenco and Michael Dregni's book on gypsy jazz. Pohren describes a Romani wedding lasting several days, which descends from party to murder as a man is knifed.[15] In Dregni's book we find a similar dichotomy of hedonism and violence, when he recounts an incident at Saintes-Maries-de-la-Mer, a place of pilgrimage for Roma, who go to venerate Saint Sarah, their patron saint. Dregni recalls hearing Django Reinhardt's music played in church, with religious lyrics set to the music.[16] But after the service fighting breaks out, and again, a man is knifed.[17] Both of these stories remind us that the gypsy figure is associated with violence and criminality as much as with music.

It is also significant that in both cases music follows the attacks. In Pohren's account, flamenco is played as part of the process of mourning for the dead man. Dregni describes how after a second knife attack music immediately strikes up as if to return a sense of normality to proceedings. We are well acquainted with the fact that the gypsy figure has long been associated with both music and violence, but it is particularly striking to see the two so closely linked in two different accounts. Gypsy music is thus presented as more than simply a specific form of music or an element of Romani culture; it is described as if it is integral to a way of life that includes other less savoury elements. These two accounts reveal that gypsy music is something whose parameters are dictated from outside of Romani society and culture – and that those parameters are not limited to the musical, but extend to perceptions of the Roma that are often inaccurate. This way of seeing and defining gypsy music transcends the styles of music that are played by and associated with the Roma.

In the example of flamenco we saw how a form of music can develop out of two cultures coexisting in one location. The music and cultures of Andalusians and Roma came together in Andalusia to result in something that could not have emerged in the way it did without input from both sides. The establishment of gypsy jazz is in some way comparable: the music of European Roma and African American jazz musicians came together in Paris to produce what is in effect a hybrid of their two musics. But whereas gypsy jazz can be regarded as a simple hybrid of musical forms, flamenco is a truer hybrid of cultures. Django Reinhardt certainly engaged with American jazz music and became embedded in the Paris jazz scene – had he not done so, gypsy jazz would not have the highly distinctive sound it does – but he first heard jazz on record and did not initially come into contact with the musicians who had been involved in jazz's gestation. It is thus a hybrid of two existing forms, which Reinhardt melded together. Flamenco, on the other hand, came about more organically, and over a more prolonged period of time, developed by two cultures that lived side by side.

The idea of the hybrid is important to gypsy music more broadly, and these models of hybridity can be applied to the Balkan gypsy music that we have already examined. The string-led music of Taraf de Haïdouks, for example, is derived from the *verbunkos* style of the Austro-Hungarian Empire, and as the conflicting viewpoints of Liszt and Bartók make clear, Hungarian folk music is an important precedent for some Balkan gypsy music. However, in some of the interpretations of classical music in their album *Maskarada* (2007), the hybridity of Taraf de Haïdouks goes even further. In their version of Bartók's 'Ostinato' from his *Mikrokosmos* (1926–39) they take a piece composed for piano and arrange it for violins and cimbaloms. They also mix this piece with snippets of one of Bartók's *Romanian Folk Dances* (1915), also composed originally for piano, but since arranged for a number of different instruments and ensembles. In their hybridization of classical music and folk music they thus draw attention to the fact that hybridization has in fact cross-pollinated these styles for many years.

The brass of Fanfare Ciocărlia is strongly informed by the brass music of the Ottoman Empire. The fact that they are drawing on a lengthy history of musical styles is evident in many of their song titles: *sirba*, *hora* and *manea* are words that recur, and all of them refer to styles of dance that were performed in the Ottoman Empire. These songs are therefore demonstrations of the band's understanding of the traditions that inform their music. But Fanfare Ciocărlia have also played their own interpretations of pieces like the James Bond theme and Steppenwolf's 'Born to Be Wild'. Their repertoire is therefore a hybrid of new and old, and of Eastern Europe and the West.

Meanwhile, electronic pop music has been a major factor in the development of *manele*, and the *manele*-derived music played by Mahala Raï Banda. However, Mahala Raï Banda are not only informed by *manele* and electronic pop. In their song 'Balkan Reggae' they apply a reggae rhythm to a piece that is otherwise informed by Balkan brass, stretching the limits of what can be typically understood as gypsy music. 'Balkan Reggae' includes gypsy-style brass and passages of cimbalom, but its distinctive rhythm places it on the fringes of what is understood as gypsy music. The song seems to be a deliberate experiment in which Mahala Raï Banda explore how far they can hybridize their music while remaining popular with fans of gypsy music.

Each of these Balkan bands is widely regarded as having brought their own gypsy style to the music they play. Whether or not there is any truth in this insistence on a not quite definable gypsy manner of playing, it is clear that when the popular perception of gypsy music is unpacked a little, it is thought of as a hybrid. Like flamenco, these Balkan styles of gypsy music have come about over a period spanning many generations, and the weight placed on tradition and authenticity in the discourses surrounding gypsy music highlights the embeddedness of the hybridization.

This might lead us to question whether all forms of gypsy music are ultimately hybrids, and whether they become more hybridized as they reach out – or are drawn out – further towards wider and more international audiences. It is arguable that Django Reinhardt would not have established gypsy jazz had he not been exposed to the music scene of Paris in the early twentieth century; had he grown up as a musician in the Balkans rather than in France his music might well have sounded very different. As we know, the environment in which it is composed and performed has a significant effect on music, and it is certain that this will remain the case when musicians go outside their native environment. The way the music of the Roma has absorbed influences depending on where they have travelled and settled is testament to this.

In an era in which most Roma are settled rather than nomadic, and in which Romani people are more likely to be immigrants than nomads, the way in which gypsy music absorbs influences has changed.[18] One significant factor in this change is that musicians now have the ability to quickly share and discover music and performance styles via the Internet. But the widespread tours that Romani musicians from the Balkans have undertaken have also no doubt informed the development, and perhaps the hybridization, of their music; this might in part be through exposure to other musicians during events such as the Gypsy Caravan tour, but the expectations of audiences and suggestions of managers are also likely to be important. It is of note that Fanfare Ciocărlia did not start to experiment with jazz sounds or cover Western popular music until they had signed to a Western label. Similarly, Taraf de Haïdouks did not engage with classical music until they became established as a gypsy world music band well known to audiences in the West.

This trend towards hybridity might open up wider audiences, but it does not necessarily have any benefits for the musicians. While some Romani performers might gain greater audiences and income as a result, the Roma remain marginalized, arguably even more so as their music is adopted by non-Romani musicians.[19] Carol Silverman has pointed out the irony that 'the hybrid often becomes a mark of authenticity (even purity), and the two terms can even be found side by side in music marketing.'[20] As we have identified, notions of authenticity are highly important in the discourse of gypsy music, and it is clear that hybridity is also important. As such, it is unsurprising that the two terms become paradoxically bound together when gypsy music is discussed and promoted. When the musicians involved are Roma, the assumptions and expectations of their audiences are very different from what they might otherwise be.

We previously considered Garth Cartwright's tenuous claims that Romani migrants to the United States, who lived alongside African Americans, might have been participants in the establishment of jazz.[21] This is certainly an attractive hypothesis, and all the more so when it is placed in the context of Django Reinhardt and gypsy jazz, and the suggestions that jazz might have emerged as a hybrid form in this way recall the development of flamenco. However, there is no evidence to suggest that Roma in the United States were involved in the formation of jazz. Yet Cartwright's idea suggests that there might be a logic of sorts in the connection between hybridity and authenticity in gypsy music. If Romani musicians play jazz then their music is invariably seen as a hybrid of jazz and gypsy music, and the fact of its hybridity might lessen its authenticity. But if an argument can be made that the Roma were involved in the early development of what is considered to be authentic jazz, then a hybrid of jazz and gypsy music would in fact be connected directly to that authenticity. Thus there is an incentive for musicians, managers and even writers to try to forge historical connections between gypsy music and other genres.

Of course, hybrids continue to be forged without any particular claims about their authenticity being made. Gypsy jazz, a hybrid form in itself, has been used as a component in further hybrids. One example is bluegrass guitarist David Grisman's album *Hot Dawg* (1978), which blends bluegrass with gypsy jazz. Its title references the Quintette du Hot Club de France and Grisman's nickname, Dawg. Bluegrass, at its core an American folk music, has also absorbed influences from jazz, so it is not in fact a particularly outlandish idea to pair it with gypsy jazz. But although the concept of an album that brings together gypsy jazz and bluegrass might seem inauthentic, *Hot Dawg* can claim some level of authenticity due to the fact that Django Reinhardt's musical partner Stéphane Grappelli plays violin on two tracks. The involvement of Grappelli indicates that authenticity is important even in gypsy music that can only be described as gypsy music in the loosest sense – neither Grappelli nor Grisman is Roma and the music is so thoroughly hybridized that any gypsiness it might claim is buried deep within layers of jazz and bluegrass.

A more recent iteration of gypsy jazz, which is also disconnected from both Romani culture and the idea of the gypsy, is apparent in the new hybrid genre of electro swing, which combines jazz and swing sounds from the era of Django Reinhardt's heyday with contemporary electronic music. Electro swing responds to nostalgia for a particular time in the same way that gypsy music, as it is marketed and consumed in the West, responds to the romanticization of the gypsy figure. With its underpinnings of electronic dance music, it has links to the similarly recent form of Balkan beats; but although Balkan beats can be thought of as a kind of contemporary gypsy music, electro swing seems too far removed from the idea of the gypsy to be described as such.

Yet in spite of the fact that there are clear limits to what can be regarded as gypsy music, it seems that the possibilities of what gypsy music can be have expanded in recent years. This can be attributed partly to the greater facility with which music crosses borders in a more globalized and technologically advanced society, and partly to the practices of Western musicians and managers tapping into a market that retains a fascination with the sense of the exotic it finds in gypsy music. Whether this stretching of gypsy music's borders is a positive thing for Romani musicians, and indeed Romani people more widely, is debatable. New forms of gypsy music imply that perceptions of the music and culture of the Roma can be broadened, and alternative and potentially more accurate perceptions of the Roma can be given greater legitimacy. However, the continued insistence on authenticity that pervades the world music and gypsy music discourses means that although the music may sound different, the stereotypes remain the same.

8 GYPSY PUNK AND BALKAN BEATS

In the Balkans, gypsy music continues to evolve. As we have seen, Balkan Romani bands have broadened their repertoires for outside audiences, encouraged by Western management, and those who perform within the region have incorporated traditional gypsy music into the electrified contemporary style of *manele*. But outside the Balkans there have also been developments; new bands and performers have gained popularity with novel hybrid forms of gypsy music aimed at Western audiences. The best known of these is Gogol Bordello, formed in New York in the late 1990s, and credited with pioneering a new form, gypsy punk.

At the centre of Gogol Bordello, and thus at the heart of gypsy punk, is Eugene Hütz. A migrant from Ukraine, he has assembled a multinational group of musicians playing a style of music with punk foundations adorned with flourishes derived from Balkan gypsy music. Hütz is a quarter Romani, but having grown up in Kiev listening to Western punk he did not discover gypsy music until he was a teenager. The first stage in his migration westwards occurred in 1986 when he moved to the Carpathian region in western Ukraine, evacuated from Kiev to stay with family after the Chernobyl disaster. There, he identified an affinity between punk and gypsy music, and the seeds of gypsy punk were sown.

On one level, Gogol Bordello operates within the tradition of New York's long-standing punk scene, adopting the discourse of politicized punk and giving wildly energetic live performances in rock venues. On another, they work within a gypsy music tradition, albeit one that is directed primarily towards Western audiences, although, as we know, this is common to much gypsy music. Hütz's guitar playing is influenced by the Russian Roma guitarist Sasha Kolpakov and the Russian gypsy guitar tradition (the Gogol Bordello songs 'Avenue B' and 'Occurrence on the Border (Hopping on a Pogo-Gypsy Stick)' borrow elements from the traditional guitar piece 'Starushka'), and the violin and accordion that are integral to the band are at times not far removed from Taraf de Haïdouks. As they have developed as a band, Gogol Bordello have absorbed other influences, notably Latin American music, but they continue to be thought of, and to present themselves, as a gypsy punk band – an indication that the idea of gypsy music can signify something more than just the music itself. As we examine gypsy punk alongside its counterpart Balkan beats, we will see that subversion and myth-making are similarly important.

While gypsy punk was beginning to coagulate in New York, something with a different sound but with a comparable cultural position was coming together in clubs in Europe. The place where this new form was birthed was a city that, like the Balkans, has a history of straddling East and West. However, while the Balkans are regarded as having provided a bridge between the civilization of Europe and the Otherness of Asia, Berlin was a divided city split between the capitalist West and communist Eastern Europe. Berlin (the city's West, at least) was a haven of counterculture even before the wall that divided it had fallen, and once Germany had been unified and, on a larger scale, the Eastern and Western sides of Europe had been drawn closer, this counterculture was in a strong position from which to grow. While the Lower East Side was the centre of New York's punk scene, its German equivalent was the district of Kreuzberg, an area of Berlin with a similar history as a centre in which immigrants settled. In common with the Lower East Side, there was a strong Jewish tradition, but while the New York district later became home to many Russians and Eastern Europeans, the next wave of immigration in Kreuzberg was primarily Turkish. Accordingly, these two areas could between them be said to have an almost Balkan population.

One migrant to Kreuzberg was a Bosnian named Robert Soko, who moved to Berlin in 1990, and began to frequent a punk bar called the Arcanoa. It was there that he began to stage the parties that grew into the Balkan beats scene. He played Balkan music and held events on socialist holidays, creating an ironic nostalgia for the recently concluded communist period of the Balkans' history, comparable with that which we have already seen in the Guča Trumpet Festival.[1] The biography produced by Soko's label, Piranha, states that he began playing Balkan rather than Western music because of 'two figures . . . [Goran] Bregović who revamped Balkan Gypsy melodies, making Balkan music palatable for a Western audience, and [Emir] Kusturica, for whose Gypsy inspired films Bregović did the soundtracks'.[2] Although Soko is not Roma himself, this is an indicator that, like many Romani musicians, he was now setting out to play for an audience of which he was not culturally a part. There is a well-established precedent of Romani musicians acting as hired performers for non-Roma, and the Eastern European based in the West occupies a similar position: he is able to reinvent the East in order to appeal to his audience. While Soko might have been reluctant to play unadulterated, or perhaps even authentic, Balkan music, he was able to court success with music that took elements from the exoticized cultures of gypsies and the Balkans but slotted neatly into the West's idea of how such music ought to sound. Balkan beats adapts gypsy music so that it is underpinned by the persistent beats heard in clubs; the bass lines are pumped out by horns playing in the style of Balkan brass bands, while the melodies played on accordion and violin offer an alternative to the repetition of techno.

Balkan beats has grown quickly; numerous compilation albums have been released and club nights catering to the style take place all over Europe. It is events like these that are marketed as Balkan or gypsy nights, where audiences are encouraged, in a clear manifestation of balkanism, to wear false moustaches and adopt a gypsy fashion. Having drawn on gypsy music and dance music, Balkan beats became influential on its own terms: it is no longer produced only by niche DJs who perform to a narrow audience. Felix Buxton of popular house act Basement Jaxx has remixed several tracks by Romani musicians, and has released Balkan beats compilations on their label, Atlantic Jaxx. In addition, the 2007 Basement Jaxx single 'Hey U' sampled Romanian brass band Fanfare Ciocărlia's song 'Asfalt Tango'. While the consumers of this music may not necessarily be aware of the nature of its source material, this is an example of a form of music usually regarded as the specialized product of gypsy music being injected into popular culture through the medium of Balkan beats.

One of the biggest names in Balkan beats is Stefan Hantel, who performs under the name Shantel. Born in Germany, and formerly a techno DJ, he developed an enthusiasm for Balkan music after he visited the Bucovina region of eastern Romania, where his family has roots. This area is very close to the Carpathian region of Ukraine, and a similarity can be drawn between Shantel and Eugene Hütz in their discoveries of gypsy music; the main difference between them is that while Hütz came to gypsy music having previously been a punk fan, Shantel had been engaged with dance music. Another difference is that while Hütz primarily plays music of his own composition, Shantel began his Balkan beats career remixing Romani bands such as Mahala Raï Banda and Fanfare Ciocărlia, and still often

covers traditional Romani songs when playing in concert. It
is perhaps for this reason that he is an unpopular figure with
Gogol Bordello, who write on their website that at one point
in their history, 'Gogol Bordello, along with Fanfare Ciocărlia,
Taraf de Haïdouks and other most progressive Gypsy bands of
Europe, get exploited by Shantel for corrupted yuppie-catored
[*sic*] Bukovina project, but cleverly breaks the ties.'[3] However, the
music and performance styles of Hütz and Shantel are certainly
comparable. While Shantel is a far more restrained performer
than the exuberant Hütz, he is similar in that he fronts and directs
a multi-ethnic group of musicians, the Bucovina Club Orkestar,
who play in a style that is informed by Romani music. Despite
his background as a DJ, Shantel acts as a frontman in his concerts,
singing and playing guitar. In a way, it is easy to see why Hütz
might feel affronted. But the accusation of exploitation seems
unfounded and almost spiteful, given that there is a common
ground of influence between the two acts. Hütz also seems

The 2009 BalkanBeats event poster created by DJ Malaka (Stefano Kappel).

Shantel (Stefan
Hantel).

confused about audience; while Gogol Bordello may be playing
to an ostensibly more working-class crowd of punk fans, to accuse
Shantel of playing for yuppies only puts him on the same stage
as the 'progressive Gypsy bands of Europe', whose audiences are
primarily Western and middle class.[4]

A more balanced and impartial critique of Shantel comes from
Ioana Szeman, who has examined his work with reference to the
Roma and the Balkans, stating that his songs 'orientalize the
Balkans from within, erasing the Roma'.[5] Her primary example
is the title track from his album *Disko Partizani* (2007), whose

lyrics 'literally suggest that by becoming Gypsy (*ţigan*) one can reach the "exotic Orient"'.[6] Szeman goes on to say that 'While Shantel may be delivering for diasporic and migrant audiences a sense of Balkan cosmopolitanism, what is troubling is what "gypsification" has come to mean in this song specifically, and in the branding of "Gypsy music" more generally.'[7] When the characteristics of the Roma are used by non-gypsy musicians, she argues, the Roma themselves are made redundant.

Shantel's appropriation of gypsy and Balkan identities continued in his 2009 album *Planet Paprika*, the follow-up to *Disko Partizani*. As a citizen of Planet Paprika, Shantel is alien in every sense of the word; in the album's title track he describes travelling to Earth on a spaceship. Planet Paprika is literally intended as another world, but the identity of Shantel's intergalactic superhero of globalization is made to be Eastern European: his homeland is named after the spice associated with Hungarian cooking and his theme song is Balkan in its style. He also declares himself to be kitsch and, as Szeman has observed, it is in being kitsch that Shantel 'gypsifies' himself.[8] Despite this, he professes not to consider that he is playing gypsy music at all: '"There is no music called Gypsy music," insists DJ Shantel. "You can only talk about traditional music from different regions in south-eastern Europe."'[9] This is an established line of argument, but the direct references to gypsies in his work, and his appropriation of Romani music, suggest that he is well aware that there is much to be gained through use of the gypsy image.

Although Balkan beats is a genre from outside the Balkans, it is comparable with styles of music from within the region. Shantel is in fact influenced by *manele*, the electronic form of gypsy music played by Romanian Roma, which is also an important influence on Mahala Raï Banda. As we discussed when considering Mahala Raï Banda's work, *manele* is considered subversive by many Romanians, and for many others this is part of its appeal. Although Shantel's Balkan beats sounds quite different from *manele*, it is one manifestation of a comparable kind of subversion: the subversive appeal of gypsy music enjoyed by Western listeners.

For Western consumers of Balkan beats, the music contains the romance of both an imagined gypsiness and also that of an imagined Balkans, and the same appeal is apparent in gypsy punk. What is significant about the Balkan beats genre specifically is that it allows us to see that the same discourses are at play in both Berlin and Bucharest. Crucially, it proves that we are not only dealing with an Orientalist, or even balkanist, dichotomy of East and West, but also with a dichotomy of Roma and non-Roma. Of course, while gypsy music in the Balkans is only subject to the latter of these distinctions, gypsy music played by Eastern Europeans in the West is tied up with both. In the Balkans, where there are much larger Roma populations than in Western Europe, gypsies are seen in a slightly different way but, as is the case in the West, they represent a less civilized East. As Szeman has pointed out, in contemporary gypsy music aimed at Western audiences, 'Gypsies are a vehicle for entering the exotic Balkans.'[10] It is arguable that the reverse is also true: the Balkans serve as a means towards encountering the gypsy other.

Although they are critical of Shantel, Gogol Bordello are certainly not opposed to the idea of Balkan beats. Pavla Fleischer's documentary film *The Pied Piper of Hützovina* (2007), which follows a journey made by Hütz through Hungary, Ukraine and Russia, includes a scene in which he plays a recording of some of his 'gypsy hip-hop' compositions to Igor Krikunov, the director of the Kiev Gypsy Theatre. Krikunov emphatically declares his opposition to this kind of music, saying that it 'harms traditional gypsy music'. Hütz is more interested in blending styles together, and has recorded material as part of his side-project, J.U.F., in collaboration with Balkan Beat Box, a New York band made up of Israeli migrants.

Since Gogol Bordello consider themselves supporters of Roma rights and brand Shantel's take on Balkan beats exploitative (this is not explained but presumably the appropriation of songs trad-itionally associated with the Roma by a musician who is not Romani is thought to be a form of exploitation), it is worthwhile comparing J.U.F. with 'Disko Partizani' and its suggestion that one can become gypsy. The most suitable song for this comparison is the first track from J.U.F.'s album *Gogol Bordello vs Tamir Muskat*, 'Gypsy Part of Town'. Both songs follow the typical Balkan beats arrangement, combining electronic beats with gypsy melodies and instrumentation, and they are both lyrically multilingual. Both begin in English; 'Disko Partizani' then introduces Romani and Romanian, while in 'Gypsy Part of Town' there are lyrics in Romani and Hebrew. In terms of music and instrumentation, there are more similarities than differences: 'Disko Partizani' is largely accordion-driven, whereas 'Gypsy Part of Town' is led by saxophone, but both include bursts of brass and saxophone solos. 'Gypsy Part of Town' is more complex, having a less standard verse–chorus structure and including a modulation, but essentially it falls within the same genre conventions as Shantel's song.

More interesting to compare are the implications of the lyrics. While 'Disko Partizani' references becoming gypsy as a desirable quality or change, the J.U.F. track brings the gypsy part of town to the fore. If Shantel is singing about becoming a gypsy while, in Szeman's words, erasing the Roma, then J.U.F. foreground gypsies. The suggestion is that an act of gypsification is taking place, but this is within the gypsy part of town, meaning that it seems to occur through infection rather than appropriation. This, combined with the use of the pejorative *gadjo* to refer to non-Roma, means that the song comes across as being narrated by a Rom, rather than by someone who is exoticizing Romani culture.

In actual fact, the 'gypsy part of town' is likely to be a slum, a ghetto or a *mahala*. Through their reference to this location, J.U.F. describe how non-Roma listeners get lost in, or become entranced by, gypsy music, in this case the *manele* of contemporary Roma. 'Gypsy Part of Town' thus shows that Balkan beats need not always entail the erasure of the Roma when elements of gypsy music are incorporated into Western styles. Whereas Shantel's 'Disko Partizani' suggests that non-Romani people can become Roma, causing the Romani people to be lost, in 'Gypsy Part of Town' the non-Roma become lost as they are drawn into a melee of multiply blended musics.

For Hütz and Gogol Bordello, the gypsy part of town is a space not unlike the immigrant melting pot of New York. In the song 'Underdog World Strike', from the album *Gypsy Punks: Underdog World Strike*, Hütz also references this imagined space, describing the various genres of music that can be heard there. While the song retains the gypsy figure and perpetuates the image of the Roma as a ghettoized group, it also breaks down certain elements of the gypsy stereotype by drawing attention to the fact that many different styles of music can be heard in Romani communities. Gogol Bordello's gypsy is not an uncivilized nomad, but the central figure in a network of musical and cultural exchange. Szeman has written that:

> As long as the 'Gypsy' stamp remains a way to exoticize any music from the Balkans, concerts and videos . . . will continue to perpetuate the romantic Gypsy stereotypes, ultimately failing to bring either the Roma or the Balkans – in their diversity and complexity – closer.[11]

What is interesting about gypsy punk is the fact that it is not simply an interpretation of Balkan music; and the gypsy of gypsy punk signifies something that is global rather than regional. Despite the derogatory nature of the word 'gypsy', it is less loaded than the word 'Balkan', with the result that, simply for reasons of nomenclature, gypsy punk is more empowering than Balkan beats.

None of Gogol Bordello are Roma themselves, though Hütz has a Romani grandparent and can thus legitimately claim some Romani identity. He has described how he has been able to further his migratory movements as a result of his ancestry; for example, he has said, 'I do utilise the Global Network of Gypsy Sofas to stay places.'[12] He has also remarked in interviews that when he moved to Rio de Janeiro in 2008, he was able to quickly associate himself with the Romani community in Brazil, implying that it was easier for him to settle there due to his connections. Discussing his move from Eastern Europe to America and then to Brazil, he has said: 'It just amazes me [that] everywhere I go I wind up hanging with family. We all know the same songs, different dialect but essentially the same language.'[13] This statement suggests a diasporic community that can transcend borders, and which does not require a national identity, and indeed, this is one way of considering Romani identity.

Gogol Bordello have not attempted to present themselves as more Romani than they are: when Hütz identifies as Roma he evidently regards this as an inherent state rather than an adopted identity, and his non-Roma colleagues have never described themselves as Roma or gypsy. However, they have not escaped criticism with regard to their handling of Roma and gypsy identities. Although they maintain an active engagement with Romani issues, for example, visiting and playing in the Turkish Roma settlement Sulukule when it was threatened with redevelopment, they have been accused of entering into the exoticizing discourse that misrepresents Romani culture. Garth Cartwright, who has championed Balkan and gypsy music extensively, makes this point as part of his criticism of the band, stating that their work 'skims the surface of Balkan Roma culture without touching on its artistry or struggle, so that it may revive several stale Gypsy clichés'.[14]

For a gypsy punk musician, however, being Roma is perhaps less important than being gypsy. A gypsy punk band made up of Romani musicians, like the Serbian group Kal, who draw closely on the culture and music of the Roma based on their own experiences as Romani people, and who use exclusively the word 'Roma' rather than 'gypsy', will receive less popular attention than a band like Gogol Bordello, who present more familiar images and ideas, even though these ideas may not necessarily be accurate.

Eugene Hütz and Sergei Ryabtsev of Gogol Bordello in Sulukule, Turkey.

This explains Hütz's need to perform gypsy identity. In order to ensure that they will be embraced by a broad audience, Gogol Bordello perform qualities associated with the stereotypical gypsy figure. Their flamboyant sense of style and their dramatic performances, during which there is a sense that all control might be lost, act as signifiers of gypsiness; combined with their self-appellation as a gypsy punk band this renders them gypsy and causes them to seem exotic and appealing.

Writing about the idea of the stranger, Sara Ahmed has noted that 'The alien stranger is . . . not beyond human, but a mechanism *for allowing us to face that which we have already designated as the beyond.'*[15] This observation can be applied to the distinction between Roma and gypsy: the Roma have been regarded as 'beyond' by many non-Roma, and the figure of the gypsy acts as a conduit through which the 'beyond' is filtered. In performing the gypsy in Gogol Bordello's music and performance, Hütz acts as an intermediary between the gypsy other and the non-Romani audience. In Ahmed's terms, he appears as a stranger through whom it is possible to face the Roma.

Hütz is an interesting figure in that he has both Romani ethnicity and the performed identity of the gypsy. He has described how 'My parents didn't want to be part of the Gypsy thing because of the baggage that it implies. They fully internalised the shame associated with being a Gypsy.'[16] Hütz has been able to escape this shame, in part through his performance of gypsy identity. When he appears with Gogol Bordello, the negative connotations associated with the gypsy figure – stereotypes of dirt and criminality – are offset by persistent associations with the exotic and the exciting. Not only does Hütz perform gypsy identity himself, he also offers consumers of gypsy punk the opportunity to become the gypsy Other through his music and performance.

Of course, this is not without its problems.[17] When non-Roma seek to become or pass as gypsy, they presume that they have come to understand the condition of being Roma. In most cases, however, they have understood the gypsy stereotype rather than the Roma. In the nineteenth century George Borrow felt that by taking on a nomadic existence and learning to speak Romani he could become gypsy; gypsy punk reaches out to a contemporary audience who hope to become gypsy by dressing in flamboyant clothing and listening to a particular kind of music. Gogol Bordello inarguably utilize the exotic connotations of the gypsy. Hütz has said in one interview:

> When you talk to gypsyologists they will always try to downplay the romantic side of the stereotype . . . But even if you downplay it, it will still be a hundred times more romantic than being a regular motherf_____.[18]

However, it should be remembered that the Romani people do not have the ability to choose to be gypsy; instead they are branded as gypsies by many non-Roma, and have to bear all of the associations carried by that term.

As musicians who draw on gypsy music influences and support Roma rights, Gogol Bordello have in their music a vessel for presenting an accurate representation of the Roma. Yet, as we have seen, their performance of the gypsy figure risks propagating stereotypes. Hütz might perform in a manner that follows the trope of exoticizing the Roma, but as a prominent figure in gypsy music, he is well placed to act as a spokesperson for the Romani people.[19] A number of Gogol Bordello's songs distance them from stereotypes, but for a band that define themselves as gypsy punk, they have included far fewer references to the Roma in their work than we might expect. It was not until the 2010 album *Trans-continental Hustle* that Romani issues were foregrounded. This album includes 'Pala Tute', which is based on a traditional Romani song, and two tracks,

'Break the Spell' and 'Trans-continental Hustle', which directly engage with the Roma.

'Break the Spell', which was originally recorded by J.U.F., is their most outspoken statement about Roma rights. This song references such issues as the practice, widespread in parts of Eastern Europe, of sending Romani children to schools for the disabled, and the fact that the Roma are accepted as musicians and entertainers but otherwise resented. The objective here seems to be to debunk exoticized versions of Romani culture and to provide detail about the realities of being Roma. This means that Gogol Bordello cannot be described as entirely guilty of perpetuating false perceptions about the Roma. Hütz's genuine interest in his Romani ethnicity and the issues facing Romani people today clearly comes across here. However, this does not continue into *Trans-continental Hustle*'s title track, which follows immediately after 'Break the Spell' on the record. In this song, we find a mythologized version of Romani history, which uses to its advantage the lack of information that most listeners have about the subject-matter. The fact that there is no definite consensus about the origins of the Roma, despite strong evidence that points towards an Indian origin, means that in 'Trans-continental Hustle' the potential for mythologizing is great.

Hütz may not intend to adopt any particular school of thought regarding the origins of the Roma, but his lyrics adhere roughly to the arguments propounded by the likes of Hancock and Lee, describing the Roma as a nomadic warrior caste. The suggestion that they were unable to acquire any territory of their own, which is presumably intended to explain their continuing nomadism and lack of national territory, seems plausible, and is certainly an appealing story. Although there is a risk of propagating false perceptions here, there is enough truth (or at least, enough of what most scholars regard as the truth) in the myth that any untrue impressions are relegated to the background.

Gogol Bordello performing live.

What is interesting about this song is that while the Roma are brought much closer to the fore than they have been in most of Gogol Bordello's previous lyrics, the music that accompanies these lyrics is moving increasingly away from the styles that are most associated with the gypsy and towards Latin American styles. This is important for two reasons. Firstly, it reminds us that gypsy music need not be confined to the sounds that might initially come to mind when the term is invoked – typically violins, accordions and minor chord progressions. Secondly, and following on from this, it encourages listeners to seek out other styles of music that are not necessarily connected directly with gypsies, and to investigate other areas of Romani music and culture.

We have considered how Hütz has Romani ethnicity but also performs a gypsy identity. The figures portrayed in 'Transcontinental Hustle' also have elements of both Roma and gypsy: they have the associations of vice and the travelling lifestyle of the much-maligned gypsy figure, but they also have the empowerment and sense of origin that is absent from representations of gypsies yet part of the culture of the Roma. One frequent misrepresentation is that the Roma do not have a sense of history.[20] This has surely contributed to the exoticism that continues to be a feature of representations of the Roma: without a history of their own, they are susceptible to having myths created on their behalf.

In performing the gypsy figure within the gypsy punk genre, Gogol Bordello might seem to be engaged in this kind of vicarious myth-making, and it is certainly the case that they interact with pre-existing myths to create a new mythology for gypsy punk. The crucial question is whether this mythology is created at the expense of the Roma. The band's forays into activism might suggest that this is not the case, but the fact that their outward focus is on music and colourful presentation means that it is difficult for them to completely avoid exoticizing the Roma. However, the myth that Gogol Bordello construct maintains enough distance between Roma and gypsy and thus does not reduce the Romani people to a romantic stereotype.

CONCLUSION

At the outset of this book I set out to answer the question: 'What is gypsy music?' Having examined just some of the styles of music that can be described with that term, it is clear that there are many ways of answering the question. It is also clear that what constitutes gypsy music is determined to a considerable extent by non-Romani and, to a growing extent, Western audiences. The figure of the gypsy is a construct that is rooted in perceptions of and stereotypes about the Romani people. Similarly, gypsy music is a construct rooted in perceptions of and stereotypes about the kind of music that Romani people play. Although gypsy music has links to the Romani people in the popular imagination and in historical and musicological discourses, it is more closely connected to the figure of the gypsy, an imaginary figure constructed from outside.

David Malvinni has suggested that in a contemporary record store we might find three forms of gypsy music, which he describes as 'the three streams of the autonomous Gypsy music bin'.[1] The first of these, he says, is concerned with ethnographic purity and follows a conception of gypsy music derived from Bartók. This is often taken to be the most typical gypsy music; it is played by Romani musicians who are typically natives of Eastern Europe and conforms to the consumer's expectations of gypsy music. But this does not necessarily mean that it is authentic by any standard other than that of the Western listener.

The second stream is described by Malvinni as 'music beyond the West', and can have its origins as far away as India.[2] It purports to relate to the movements taken by the Roma from Rajasthan to Eastern Europe, and it therefore contains elements taken from various stopping places along this route.

The final category, 'gypsy world music', is said to be 'produced with the burgeoning world-music audience in mind as intended listeners and buyers'.[3] The two examples that Malvinni cites here are Kalyi Jag and Csókolom, both Hungarian bands who play from a traditional gypsy music repertoire, adding inflections from popular music. All three of the contemporary Romanian bands considered in this book – Taraf de Haïdouks, Fanfare Ciocărlia and Mahala Raï Banda – could also be thought of as part of the 'gypsy world music' category: they have been marketed in the West with specific audiences in mind, and have become firmly fixed in the world music scene by the introduction of hybrid elements to their work.

We can distinguish between the hybridized gypsy music of Taraf de Haïdouks and Fanfare Ciocărlia, who have been encouraged to deviate into hybrid forms by their labels, and the hybrids performed by Django Reinhardt and Gogol Bordello, who both combine styles of music that they have encountered more organically. However, their audiences overlap considerably, drawn to the music by the elements of gypsiness that they present. It is as though the scales, intervals and flourishes that have come to signify gypsiness act like a dominant gene in the music's DNA; whether they are combined with jazz, punk or classical music, the resulting sound is invariably understood to be a kind of gypsy music.

There are arguments that the notion of gypsiness and the idea of the gypsy have evolved in parallel with gypsy music. Malvinni has observed that

> Gypsiness in music, which in the nineteenth century meant
> the carefree attitude of the suffering Gypsy fiddler, has
> perhaps recently undergone a broadening to include migrant
> categories such as the refugee. In other words, Gypsiness in
> music today has become an intensely politicized category.[4]

It is arguable that this has always been the case: Romani musicians
played in a state of servitude in the Balkans, flamenco was founded
in a climate of hostility towards migrants in Spain, and the place
of gypsy music in Soviet Russia was bound up with notions of
Soviet citizenship that informed the way the music was played
and performed.

In the contemporary environment, Malvinni's point that
gypsiness in music is increasingly politicized is particularly
relevant to gypsy punk: this is not only because of the changing
profile of the Romani people, but also due to the fact that the
figure of the gypsy is now being used by musicians to signify
more than simply the traditional stereotype of the gypsy figure.
In the case of Gogol Bordello's gypsy punk, the gypsy is used as
an access route into discourses about migration: Eugene Hütz's
identity as an immigrant is as important to him as his identity
as a Rom, and the majority of the band's other musicians are
non-Roma who are immigrants in the u.s. The gypsy and the
immigrant are both prominent Others, and it is not surprising
that the gypsy figure should find itself linked to parallel Others
as gypsy music evolves; this is something that we have also seen
in discussions of gypsy music and jazz, with Roma and African
Americans seen as connected through music.

The example of gypsy punk also reveals something that
is common to many forms of gypsy music: the notion of
gypsiness is more important to its reception than whether it
is actually performed by Romani musicians. Authenticity has
been a recurring concern throughout our investigation of gypsy

music but, in the context of gypsy music, it does not always signify what we might expect it to. Since before Liszt wrote his treatise on gypsy music there has been a school of thought that unadulterated gypsy music performed by Romani musicians who have not absorbed outside influences is more authentic. But it should by now be clear that no gypsy music can be described as pure or unadulterated, and that hybridity is endemic to it. The notion of the authentic is thus an illusion when applied to gypsy music – though it is frequently applied to gypsy music by those who sell it.

Gypsy music has historically been associated with certain locations, and the Balkans remain a focal point for much contemporary gypsy music. However, the emergence of new gypsy music forms, such as Balkan beats and gypsy punk, shows that globalized major cities like Berlin and New York can also be fertile spaces for gypsy music production. The division between rural tradition and urban hybridity and change is something that we have encountered in long-standing perceptions of gypsy music, and while the villages of Romania remain appealing as sites of concentrated musical activity, it seems likely that further innovations in gypsy music are likely to come about in cities, both within and outside of the Balkans. But wherever new styles of gypsy music are developed, it seems unlikely that the allure of the exotic gypsy figure and the comparable appeal of the Balkans will be absent from their supporting mythology. It might seem regressive for these perceptions and stereotypes to persist, but it is possible that newer forms of gypsy music, perhaps those spearheaded by Romani musicians rather than by Western promoters, will address the desire for gypsiness in novel ways that provide a fairer and more nuanced portrayal of the Roma.

REFERENCES

INTRODUCTION

1 Franz Liszt, *The Gipsy in Music*, trans. Edwin Evans (London, 1926), p. 139.
2 Jon Pareles, 'The Whole World Gets Into the Groove', *New York Times* (14 January 2014), p. C1.
3 Edward W. Said, *Orientalism* [1978] (London, 2003), p. 1.
4 Misha Glenny does not include Slovenia in his history, though he does include every other country that can be conceived of as Balkan. This is the same mapping as that used by Maria Todorova.
5 Christopher Cviic, in *Remaking the Balkans* (London, 1991), excluded both Greece and Turkey from his study on the grounds that they had not been communist-controlled. However, he does describe them as 'Balkan countries'. Robert Bideleux and Ian Jeffries, in *The Balkans: A Post-communist History* (Abingdon, 2007), also exclude these countries from their rather Eurocentric post-communist history of the Balkans, citing the same reason for omitting Greece, although they do not comment on Turkey. They also exclude Slovenia, describing it as 'more "East Central European" than "Balkan"'.
6 Sarah Houghton-Walker, *Representations of the Gypsy in the Romantic Period* (Oxford, 2014), p. 12.
7 Angus Fraser, *The Gypsies* (Oxford, 1992), p. 1.
8 Ian Hancock, *We Are the Romani People* (Hatfield, 2002), p. xx.
9 Wim Willems, *In Search of the True Gypsy*, trans. Don Bloch (London, 1997), p. 7.
10 Ibid., p. 5.
11 Hancock, *We Are the Romani People*, p. xvii.
12 Ibid.
13 'Making Human Rights for Roma a Reality', www.coe.int, 19 October 2015.
14 Zoltan Barany, *The East European Gypsies* (Cambridge, 2002), p. 103.
15 Alaina Lemon, *Between Two Fires* (Durham, NC, 2000), p. 3.

16 Ibid.
17 Kalwant Bhopal and Martin Myers, *Insiders, Outsiders and Others: Gypsies and Identity* (Hatfield, 2008), p. 20.
18 Houghton-Walker, *Representations of the Gypsy*, p. 9.
19 Katie Trumpener, 'The Time of the Gypsies: A "People without History" in the Narratives of the West', *Critical Inquiry*, XVIII/4 (1992), p. 869.
20 Emily Brontë, *Wuthering Heights* [1847] (Harmondsworth, 1980), p. 47.
21 For a comprehensive account of fictional representations of the gypsy in Europe, see Max Peter Baumann, 'The Reflection of the Roma in European Art Music', *World of Music*, XXXVIII/1 (1996), pp. 95–138.
22 Miguel de Cervantes Saavedra, *La Gitanilla*, trans. John Ozell (London, 1709), p. 1.
23 Mérimée is partly informed by the work of George Borrow. The final chapter of *Carmen* provides contextual information about the 'bohémiens' of Spain, in which Mérimée provides a typical description of the 'gypsies' as a swarthy race who make their living my driving mules and begging, and cites Borrow's descriptions of the Roma in Spain, in *The Bible in Spain* (London, 1843), as a source.
24 Prosper Mérimée, *Carmen*, in *Romans et Nouvelles*, vol. II (Paris, 1967), p. 359.
25 Ibid., p. 360.
26 Ibid., p. 402.
27 Ibid., p. 401.
28 Alexander Pushkin, *The Gypsies* [1827], trans. Antony Wood (London, 2006), p. 3.
29 Ibid., p. 4.
30 Ibid.
31 Michael Holroyd, *Augustus John* (London, 1996), p. 103.
32 Augustus John, 'Letter to John Rothenstein' (14 May 1952), cited ibid., p. 27.
33 Willems, *In Search of the True Gypsy*, p. 100.
34 Jimi Hendrix, *Starting at Zero: His Own Story* (London, 2013), p. 217.
35 Isabel Fonseca, *Bury Me Standing: The Gypsies and Their Journey* (London, 1995), p. 15.
36 Garth Cartwright, *Princes Amongst Men: Journeys with Gypsy Musicians* (London, 2005), p. 4.

1 THE ORIGINS OF BALKAN GYPSY MUSIC

1 Ian Hancock, 'Origins of the Romani People', www.reocities.com, 17 April 1999.
2 Ronald Lee, 'A New Look at our Romani Origins and Diaspora', www.kopachi.com, 2009.
3 Ian Hancock, *We Are the Romani People* (Hatfield, 2002), p. 1.
4 Angus Fraser, *The Gypsies* (Oxford, 1992), p. 58; Ian Hancock, *The Pariah Syndrome* (Ann Arbor, MI, 1987), p. 16.
5 David Crowe, 'The Gypsy Historical Experience in Romania', in *The Gypsies of Eastern Europe*, ed. David Crowe and John Kolsti (London, 1991), p. 61.
6 Fraser, *The Gypsies*, p. 131. For a more detailed catalogue of laws passed against the Roma and other forms of persecution, see Hancock's *The Pariah Syndrome*.
7 Fraser, *The Gypsies*, p. 226.
8 Hancock, *We Are the Romani People*, p. 34.
9 Zoltan Barany, *The East European Gypsies* (Cambridge, 2002), p. 103.
10 Gilad Margalit, *Germany and its Gypsies* (Madison, WI, 2002), p. 83.
11 This is not a policy that is confined to either communism or Eastern Europe; regulations in the United Kingdom, for example, have made it increasingly difficult for Roma to travel and, as a result, many have become settled.
12 Fraser, *The Gypsies*, p. 157.
13 Angus Bancroft, *Roma and Gypsy-travellers in Europe* (Aldershot, 2005), p. 29.
14 Barany, *The East European Gypsies*, p. 120.
15 Ian Traynor, 'Apartheid in the Heart of Europe: How Roma Children Lose Out on Education', *The Guardian* (16 November 2007), p. 25.
16 Nicholas Kulish, 'As Economic Turmoil Mounts, So Do Deadly Attacks on Hungary's Gypsies', *New York Times* (26 April 2009), p. A1. For a more in-depth (though less up-to-date) account of the situation of Hungarian Roma, see Rachel Guglielmo and Timothy Waters, *Rights Denied: The Roma of Hungary* (New York, 1996).
17 Aidan Lewis, 'Italy Torn by Racial Strains', news.bbc.co.uk, 4 February 2009.
18 'France sends Roma Gypsies back to Romania', news.bbc.co.uk, 20 August 2010.
19 Conor Lally, 'Gardaí say More Roma in Line to be Deported', *Irish Times* (17 August 2007), p. 4.
20 Rachel Stevenson, 'Dale Farm Travellers: We Won't Just Get Up and Leave', *The Guardian* (27 July 2010), G2, p. 13.

21 For a more in-depth investigation of portrayals of Roma in the British media, see Kalwant Bhopal and Martin Myers, *Insiders, Outsiders and Others: Gypsies and Identity* (Hatfield, 2008), pp. 145–74. Herein representations of 'gypsies' in *The Sun* and *The Independent* in 2005 are analysed.

22 Mark Reynolds, 'Gypsy in £3m Benefit Fiddle', *Daily Express* (27 July 2010), p. 1. For a comprehensive survey of anti-Romani incidents in Europe in the late twentieth and early twenty-first centuries, see Yaron Matras, *I Met Lucky People: The Story of the Romani Gypsies* (London, 2014), pp. 193–206.

23 Barany, *The East European Gypsies*, p. 207.

24 Bernard Rorke and Orhan Usein, ed., *A Lost Decade: Reflections on Roma Inclusion, 2005–2015* (Budapest, 2015).

25 Derek Hawes and Barbara Perez, *The Gypsy and the State: The Ethnic Cleansing of British Society* (Bristol, 1995), p. 144.

26 Alaina Lemon, *Between Two Fires* (Durham, NC, 2000), p. 3.

27 Although, as Ian Hancock points out, many Roma slaves were not permitted to play for their own amusement. See Hancock, *The Pariah Syndrome*, pp. 18–20.

28 Becky Taylor, *Another Darkness, Another Dawn: A History of Gypsies, Roma and Travellers* (London, 2014), p. 37.

29 Carol Silverman, *Romani Routes: Cultural Politics and Balkan Music in Diaspora* (Oxford, 2012), p. 21.

30 Fraser, *The Gypsies*, p. 35.

31 Hancock, *We Are the Romani People*, p. 5.

32 Carol Silverman, 'Rom (Gypsy) Music', in *The Garland Encyclopedia of World Music*, vol. VIII: *Europe*, ed. Timothy Rice, James Porter and Chris Goertzen (New York, 2000), p. 277.

33 Ibid.

34 Ibid., p. 270.

35 Ibid., pp. 278, 280.

36 Garth Cartwright, *Princes Amongst Men: Journeys with Gypsy Musicians* (London, 2005), p. 44.

37 A. L. Lloyd, 'The Music of Rumanian Gypsies', *Proceedings of the Royal Musical Association*, XC (1963–4), p. 15.

38 Ibid., p. 21.

39 Carol Silverman, 'Music and Power: Gender and Performance Among Roma (Gypsies) of Skopje, Macedonia', *World of Music*, XXXVIII/1 (1996), p. 69.

40 Mattijs van de Port, 'The Articulation of Soul: Gypsy Musicians and the Serbian Other', *Popular Music*, XXVIII/3 (1999), p. 292.

41 Mattijs van de Port, 'Outstanding Musicians and the Stranger Within: Reflections on Serb Perceptions of Gypsy Music', *Etnofoor*, x/1 (1997), p. 9.
42 Ibid., p. 10.
43 Cartwright, *Princes Amongst Men*, p. 43.
44 Ibid., p. 45.
45 Margaret H. Beissinger, 'Occupation and Ethnicity: Constructing Identity among Professional Romani (Gypsy) Musicians in Romania', *Slavic Review*, lx/1 (2001), p. 26.
46 Julia Heuwekemeijer, 'Taraf de Haïdouks as Re-gypsyfiers: A Critique on the Seductions of Authenticity', http://culturalmusicology.org, accessed 26 October 2015.
47 Ibid.
48 Ibid.
49 Simon Frith, 'Towards an Aesthetic of Popular Music', in *Music and Society: The Politics of Composition, Performance and Reception*, ed. Richard Leppert and Susan McClary (Cambridge, 1987), p. 136.

2 LISZT VS BARTÓK: THE HUNGARIAN QUESTION

1 Lynn M. Hooker, *Redefining Hungarian Music from Liszt to Bartók* (Oxford, 2013), pp. 35–6.
2 Shay Loya, *Liszt's Transcultural Modernism and the Hungarian-gypsy Tradition* (Rochester, NY, 2011), pp. 60–61.
3 Barbara Rose Lange, '"What Was That Conquering Magic . . .": The Power of Discontinuity in Hungarian Gypsy Nóta', *Ethnomusicology*, xli/3 (Autumn 1997), pp. 517–37.
4 Jonathan Bellman, 'Toward a Lexicon for the *Style Hongrois*', *Journal of Musicology*, ix/2 (Spring 1991), pp. 214–37.
5 Franz Liszt, *The Gipsy in Music*, trans. Edwin Evans (London, 1926), p. 300.
6 Loya, *Liszt's Transcultural Modernism*, p. 9.
7 Ibid.
8 Carol Silverman, *Romani Routes: Cultural Politics and Balkan Music in Diaspora* (Oxford, 2012), pp. 27, 301.
9 Ibid., p. 29.
10 Liszt, *The Gipsy in Music*, p. 292.
11 Ibid.
12 Ibid., p. 270.
13 Ibid., p. 8.

14 Ibid., p. 12.
15 Ibid., p. 13.
16 Ibid., p. 91.
17 Loya, *Liszt's Transcultural Modernism*, p. 58.
18 Liszt, *The Gipsy in Music*, p. 270.
19 Ibid., p. 269.
20 Hooker, *Redefining Hungarian Music*, pp. 70–78.
21 Loya, *Liszt's Transcultural Modernism*, p. 100.
22 David Malvinni, *The Gypsy Caravan: From Real Roma to Imaginary Gypsies in Western Music and Film* (New York, 2004), p. 10.
23 Béla Bartók, 'Gipsy Music or Hungarian Music?', in *Béla Bartók Essays*, ed. Benjamin Suchoff (Lincoln, NE, 1992), p. 206.
24 Ibid., p. 222.
25 Hooker, *Redefining Hungarian Music*, p. 96.
26 Julie Brown, 'Bartók, the Gypsies and Hybridity in Music', in *Western Music and its Others*, ed. Georgia Born and David Hesmondhalgh (Berkeley, CA, 2000), p. 119.
27 Béla Bartók, 'The Bartók-Möller Polemical Interchange', in *Béla Bartók Studies in Ethnomusicology*, ed. Benjamin Suchoff (Lincoln, NE, 1992), p. 144.
28 Brown, 'Bartók, the Gypsies and Hybridity in Music', p. 123.
29 Ibid., p. 131.
30 Malvinni, *The Gypsy Caravan*, p. 8.
31 A. L. Lloyd, 'The Music of Rumanian Gypsies', *Proceedings of the Royal Musical Association*, XC (1963–4), p. 19.
32 Simon Frith, 'Towards an Aesthetic of Popular Music', in *Music and Society: The Politics of Composition, Performance and Reception*, ed. Richard Leppert and Susan McClary (Cambridge, 1987), p. 138.
33 Bálint Sárosi, *Gypsy Music*, trans. Fred Macnicol (Budapest, 1978), p. 23.
34 Malvinni, *The Gypsy Caravan*, p. 158.
35 Ibid.
36 Ibid., p. xi.
37 Silverman, *Romani Routes*, p. 51.
38 Ibid., p. 261.
39 Malvinni appears to use the word Roma in quotes here in order to acknowledge its relatively recent widespread adoption; in the remainder of the text he uses it without quotes; Malvinni, *The Gypsy Caravan*, p. ix.

3 GYPSY MUSIC AND BALKANISM

1 It has also been alleged that Kusturica's work, particularly his 1995 film *Underground*, which deals with the conflict in Yugoslavia in the early 1990s, takes a particularly Serbian stance. Amongst the most outspoken of Kusturica's critics is Alain Finkielkraut. See Finkielkraut, 'L'imposture Kusturica', *Le Monde* (2 June 1995), p. 16; quotation from Dina Iordanova, *Emir Kusuturica* (London, 2002), p. 6.

2 Goran Gocić, *Notes From the Underground: The Cinema of Emir Kusturica* (London, 2001), p. 114.

3 Ioana Szeman, '"Gypsy Music" and Deejays: Orientalism, Balkanism and Romani Musicians', *TDR: The Drama Review*, LIII/3 (Autumn 2009), p. 103.

4 Ibid.

5 Gocić, *Notes From the Underground*, p. 112.

6 Maria Todorova, *Imagining the Balkans* (Oxford, 2009), p. 7.

7 Ibid., p. 21.

8 Ibid., p. 194.

9 Milica Bakić-Hayden, 'Nesting Orientalisms', *Slavic Review*, LIV/4 (Winter 1995), p. 917.

10 Todorova, *Imagining the Balkans*, p. 12.

11 Ibid., p. 3.

12 Misha Glenny, 'Only in the Balkans', *London Review of Books*, XXI/9 (29 April 1999), p. 12.

13 Ibid.

14 Todorova, *Imagining the Balkans*, pp. 15–16.

15 Ibid., p. 58.

16 Slavoj Žižek, '"You May!"', *London Review of Books*, XXI/6 (18 March 1999), p. 3.

17 'Balkanize, v', http://dictionary.oed.com, accessed 26 October 2015.

18 Mark Mazower, *The Balkans* (London, 2000), p. 48. See also pp. 104–27 for further discussion on heterogeneity and the construction of nation states in the Balkans.

19 Robert Bideleux and Ian Jeffries, *The Balkans: A Post-communist History* (Abingdon, 2007), p. xii.

20 Elena Mariushiakova and Vesselin Popov: 'The Roma – A Nation Without a State? Historical Background and Contemporary Tendencies', in *Nationalisms Across the Globe: An Overview of Nationalisms in State-endowed and Stateless Nations,* ed. Wojciech J. Burszta, Tomasz Kamusella and Sebastian Wojciechowski (Poznan, 2005), p. 438.

21 William Howard-Flanders, *Balkania* (London, 1909), p. 99.

22 Bideleux and Jeffries, *The Balkans*, p. 8.
23 Ibid., p. 14.
24 Misha Glenny, *The Balkans* (London, 1999), p. xxiv.
25 Yonka Krasteva, 'Western Writing and the (Re)Construction of the Balkans After 1989: The Bulgarian Case', in *The Balkans and the West*, ed. Andrew Hammond (Oxford, 2004), p. 97.
26 Zoltan Barany, *The East European Gypsies* (Cambridge, 2002), p. 139.

4 CONTEMPORARY GYPSY MUSIC IN THE BALKANS

1 Ludwig Wittgenstein, *Philosophical Investigations*, trans. G.E.M. Anscombe (Oxford, 1963), p. 32.
2 Martin Stokes, 'Music and the Global Order', *Annual Review of Anthropology*, XXXIII (2004), p. 52; Simon Frith, 'The Discourse of World Music', in *Western Music and Its Others*, ed. Georgina Born and David Hesmondhalgh (Berkeley, CA, 2000), p. 305.
3 Rupa Huq, *Beyond Subculture* (London, 2006), p. 64.
4 Frith, 'The Discourse of World Music', p. 307.
5 Wilfred Raussert, 'Introduction: Traveling Sounds: Music, Migration and Identity Formation', in *Traveling Sounds: Music, Migration and Identity in the U.S. and Beyond*, ed. Wilfred Raussert and John Miller Jones (Berlin, 2008), p. 12.
6 Jocelyne Guilbault, 'On Redefining the "Local" Through World Music', in *Ethnomusicology: A Contemporary Reader*, ed. Jennifer C. Post (New York, 2006), p. 142.
7 Carol Silverman, 'Rom (Gypsy) Music', in *The Garland Encyclopedia of World Music*, vol. VIII: *Europe*, ed. Timothy Rice, James Porter and Chris Goertzen (New York, 2000), p. 274.
8 David Malvinni, *The Gypsy Caravan: From Real Roma to Imaginary Gypsies in Western Music and Film* (New York, 2004), p. 249.
9 Ibid., p. 250.
10 Chris Nickson, 'Taraf de Haïdouks', http://worldmusic.nationalgeographic.com, accessed 10 July 2012.
11 Garth Cartwright, *Princes Amongst Men: Journeys with Gypsy Musicians* (London, 2005), p. 188.
12 Garth Cartwright, 'Obituary: Nicolae Neacsu: Romanian Gypsy Violinist Who Conquered the West', *The Guardian* (16 September 2002), p. 20.
13 Jean-Stéphane Brosse, sleeve notes to *Maskarada* (1997).

14 Ibid.

15 Cartwright, *Princes Amongst Men*, p. 214.

16 Ioana Szeman, '"Gypsy Music" and Deejays: Orientalism, Balkanism and Romani Musicians', *TDR: The Drama Review*, LIII/3 (Autumn 2009), p. 100.

17 Garth Cartwright, sleeve notes to *Gili Garabdi* (2005).

18 Cartwright, *Princes Amongst Men*, p. 48.

19 'Boban and Marko Marković Orchestra vs Fanfare Ciocărlia', www.asphalt-tango.de, accessed 26 October 2015.

20 Beissinger has suggested that these areas existed, and were inhabited by gypsy musicians, as far back as the sixteenth century. See Margaret H. Beissinger, *The Art of the Lăutar: The Epic Tradition of Romania* (New York, 1991), p. 18.

21 Cristina Mosora, 'Manele the New Balkan Reggaeton', www.bridge-mag. com, accessed 10 July 2012.

22 Margaret H. Beissinger, '*Muzică Orientală*: Identity and Popular Culture in Postcommunist Romania', in *Balkan Popular Culture and the Ottoman Ecumene*, ed. Donna A. Buchanan (Lanham, MD, 2007), p. 101.

23 Ibid., p. 117

24 Ibid., p. 97.

25 Garth Cartwright, 'Blowing Up a Storm', *The Independent* (5 May 2006), Arts and Book Review, p. 3.

26 'Mahala Rai Banda', www.asphalt-tango.de, accessed 26 October 2015.

27 Lucia Udvardyova, 'Eastern Haze: December 2013', www.electronicbeats.net, accessed 26 October 2015.

28 Margaret H. Beissinger, 'The Performance of "Oriental Music" in Contemporary Romania', in *Ethnic Identities in Dynamic Perspective*, ed. Sheila Salo and Csaba Prónai (Budapest, 2003), p. 230.

5 GYPSY MUSIC IN RUSSIA

1 Gerald Stanton Smith, *Songs to Seven Strings: Russian Guitar Poetry and Soviet Mass Song* (Bloomington, IN, 1984), p. 61.

2 Alaina Lemon, *Between Two Fires* (Durham, NC, 2000), p. 22.

3 Brigid O'Keeffe, *New Soviet Gypsies: Nationality, Performance, and Selfhood in the Early Soviet Union* (Toronto, 2013), p. 31.

4 Ibid., p. 33.

5 Ibid., p. 34.

6 Franz Liszt, *The Gipsy in Music*, trans. Edwin Evans (London, 1926), pp. 151–3.

7 Ibid., p. 155.

8   O'Keeffe, *New Soviet Gypsies*, p. 5.

9   Becky Taylor, *Another Darkness, Another Dawn: A History of Gypsies, Roma and Travellers* (London, 2014), p. 160.

10 Zoltan Barany, *The East European Gypsies* (Cambridge, 2002), p. 114.

11 O'Keeffe, *New Soviet Gypsies*, p. 14.

12 Lemon, *Between Two Fires*, p. 22.

13 Stanton Smith, *Songs to Seven Strings*, p. 61.

14 Alexander Kuprin, 'On the Passing of the Gypsy Song in Russia', *Lotus Magazine*, VIII/9 (June 1917), p. 407.

15 Alaina Lemon, 'Roma (Gypsies) in the USSR and the Moscow Teatr "Romen"', in *Gypsies: An Interdisciplinary Reader*, ed. Diane Tong (New York, 1998), p. 150.

16 Lemon, *Between Two Fires*, p. 11.

17 Oleg Timofeyev and Marco Bazzotti, 'The Seven-string Guitar in 19th-century Russian Culture', *Il Fronimo*, CIII (1998), pp. 27–40.

18 Ibid.

19 Oleg Timofeyev, 'The Golden Age of the Russian Guitar: Repertoire, Performance Practice, and Social Function of the Russian Seven-string Guitar Music, 1800–1850', PhD thesis, Duke University, 1999.

20 Stanton Smith, *Songs to Seven Strings*, p. 60.

21 Ibid., p. 1.

22 Ibid., pp. 1, 63–4.

23 Brian A. Horne, 'The Bards of Magnitizdat', in *Samizdat, Tamizdat, and Beyond*, ed. Friederike Kind-Kovacs and Jessie Labov (New York, 2013), p. 182.

24 Ibid., p. 183.

25 Alaina Lemon, 'Hot Blood and Black Pearls: Socialism, Society, and Authenticity at the Moscow Teatr Romen', *Theatre Journal*, XLVIII/4 (December 1996), p. 480.

26 Horne, 'The Bards of Magnitizdat', p. 182.

27 David Malvinni, *The Gypsy Caravan: From Real Roma to Imaginary Gypsies in Western Music and Film* (New York, 2004), pp. 115–17.

6 GYPSY MUSIC IN SPAIN: FLAMENCO

1   D. E. Pohren, *The Art of Flamenco* (Sevilla, 1967), p. 43; Peter Manuel, 'Andalusian, Gypsy, and Class Identity in the Contemporary Flamenco Complex', *Ethnomusicology*, XXXIII/1 (Winter 1993), p. 50.

2   Pohren, *The Art of Flamenco*, pp. 36–8.

3   Timothy Mitchell, *Flamenco Deep Song* (New Haven, CT, 1994), p. 4.

4   Pohren, *The Art of Flamenco*, p. 46.

5   Ibid., p. 15; Bernard Leblon, *Gypsies and Flamenco: The Emergence of the Art of Flamenco in Andalusia* (Hatfield, 2000), p. 43.

6   Pohren, *The Art of Flamenco*, p. 47.

7   Mitchell, *Flamenco Deep Song*, p. 2.

8   Pohren, *The Art of Flamenco*, pp. 97–8.

9   Ibid., p. 99.

10 William Washabaugh, *Flamenco Music and National Identity in Spain* (Farnham, 2012), p. 5.

11 Leblon, *Gypsies and Flamenco*, p. 72.

12 Ibid., p. 73.

13 'Flamenco', www.unesco.org, accessed 26 October 2015.

14 George Borrow, *The Zincali* (London, 1841), p. 39; Leblon, *Gypsies and Flamenco*, p. 14.

15 Ibid.

16 Becky Taylor, *Another Darkness, Another Dawn: A History of Gypsies, Roma and Travellers* (London, 2014), p. 67; Leblon, *Gypsies and Flamenco*, pp. 17–31.

17 Ibid., pp. 42, 43.

18 Pohren, *The Art of Flamenco*, p. 36.

19 Ibid.

20 Mitchell, *Flamenco Deep Song*, p. 51.

21 Judith Okely, *The Traveller-gypsies* (Cambridge, 1983).

22 Mitchell, *Flamenco Deep Song*, p. 41.

23 Manuel, 'Andalusian, Gypsy, and Class Identity', p. 184.

24 Bertha B. Quintana, '"The Duende Roams Freely This Night": An Analysis of an Interethnic Event in Granada, Spain', in *Gypsies: An Interdisciplinary Reader*, ed. Diane Tong (New York, 1998), pp. 167–71.

25 Federico García Lorca, 'Play and Theory of the Duende', in *In Search of Duende*, ed. and trans. Christopher Maurer (New York, 1998), pp. 48–62.

26 Christopher Maurer, 'Introduction', in Federico García Lorca, *Selected Poems*, (London, 1997), p. xi.

27 Manuel, 'Andalusian, Gypsy, and Class Identity', p. 195.

28 Andrew Brown, 'Introduction', in Prosper Mérimée, *Carmen* (London, 2004), p. xiii.

29 José F. Colmeiro, 'Exorcising Orientalism: *Carmen* and the Construction of Oriental Spain', *Comparative Literature* LIV/2 (Spring 2002), p. 127.

30 Ibid., p. 143.

31 George Borrow, *The Bible in Spain* (London, 1843), p. 306.
32 Leblon, *Gypsies and Flamenco*, p. 43.
33 Maria Todorova, *Imagining the Balkans* (Oxford, 2009), p. 7.
34 Colmeiro, 'Exorcising Orientalism', p. 129.
35 Ibid.
36 Eva Woods Peiró, *White Gypsies: Race and Stardom in Spanish Musicals* (Minneapolis, MN, 2012), p. 24.

7 GYPSY JAZZ: HYBRID FORMS

1   Michael Dregni, *Django: The Life and Music of a Gypsy Legend* (Oxford, 2004), p. 13.
2   Benjamin Givan, 'Django Reinhardt's Left Hand', in *Jazz Planet*, ed. E. Taylor Atkins (Jackson, MS, 2003), p. 21.
3   Dregni, *Django*, p. 73.
4   Ibid., p. 10.
5   Givan, 'Django Reinhardt's Left Hand', p. 20.
6   Dregni, *Django*, p. 64.
7   Ibid., p. 87.
8   Hugues Panassié, *The Real Jazz*, trans. Anne Sorelle Williams (New York, 1942), pp. 143–4.
9   Andy Fry, *Paris Blues: African American Music and French Popular Culture* (Chicago, IL, 2014), p. 210.
10 Givan, 'Django Reinhardt's Left Hand', p. 22.
11 Ibid., p. 39.
12 Franz Liszt, *The Gipsy in Music*, trans. Edwin Evans (London, 1926), p. 8.
13 Fry, *Paris Blues*, p. 175.
14 Tony Whyton, *Jazz Icons* (Cambridge, 2010), p. 113.
15 D. E. Pohren, *The Art of Flamenco* (Sevilla, 1967), p. 27.
16 Dregni, *Django*, p. 135.
17 Ibid., p. 139.
18 See Yaron Matras, *I Met Lucky People: The Story of the Romani Gypsies* (London, 2014), p. 33.
19 Carol Silverman, *Romani Routes: Cultural Politics and Balkan Music in Diaspora* (Oxford, 2012), p. 45.
20 Ibid., p. 46.
21 Garth Cartwright, *Princes Amongst Men: Journeys with Gypsy Musicians* (London, 2005), p. 48.

8 GYPSY PUNK AND BALKAN BEATS

1   'Robert Soko: Biography', www.piranha.de, accessed 26 October 2015.
2   Ibid.
3   'A Brief History of Gogol Bordello', www.gogolbordello.com, accessed
    10 July 2012.
4   For audience demographics, see Carol Silverman, 'Trafficking in the Exotic
    with "Gypsy" Music: Balkan Roma, Cosmopolitanism, and "World Music"
    Festivals', in *Balkan Popular Culture and the Ottoman Ecumene*, ed. Donna A.
    Buchanan (Lanham, MD, 2007), p. 348.
5   Ioana Szeman, '"Gypsy Music" and Deejays: Orientalism, Balkanism and
    Romani Musicians', *TDR: The Drama Review*, LIII/3 (Autumn 2009), p. 100.
6   Ibid.
7   Ibid., p. 114.
8   Ibid., p. 113.
9   Dorian Lynskey, 'There is No Such Thing as Gypsy Music', *The Guardian*
    (24 November 2006), Features, p. 5.
10 Szeman, '"Gypsy Music" and Deejays', p. 100.
11 Ibid., p. 114.
12 'A Round with Gogol Bordello's Eugene Hütz', *Q Magazine* (April 2008),
    p. 30.
13 Julie Garisto, 'Gogol Bordello's Eugene Hütz Talks Gypsy Rock, Recording
    with Rick Rubin', http://blogs.tampabay.com, 23 July 2009.
14 Garth Cartwright, 'Blowing Up a Storm', *The Independent* (5 May 2006),
    Arts and Books Review, p. 3.
15 Sara Ahmed, *Strange Encounters: Embodied Others in Post-coloniality*
    (London, 2000), p. 3.
16 'A Round with Gogol Bordello's Eugene Hütz', p. 30.
17 Ahmed, *Strange Encounters*, p. 133.
18 Hugh Porter, 'Immigrant Punk: Eugene Hütz', www.time.com,
    13 August 2008.
19 Carol Silverman, *Romani Routes: Cultural Politics and Balkan Music in Diaspora*
    (Oxford, 2012), p. 287.
20 See Zoltan Barany, *The East European Gypsies* (Cambridge, 2002), p. 205,
    and Isabel Fonseca, *Bury Me Standing: The Gypsies and Their Journey* (London,
    1995), p. 243, for examples of this.

CONCLUSION

1   David Malvinni, *The Gypsy Caravan: From Real Roma to Imaginary Gypsies in Western Music and Film* (New York, 2004), p. 208.
2   Ibid., p. 209.
3   Ibid., p. 210.
4   Ibid., p. 65.

BIBLIOGRAPHY

Ahmed, Sara, *Strange Encounters: Embodied Others in Post-coloniality* (London, 2000)

Bakić-Hayden, Milica, 'Nesting Orientalisms', *Slavic Review*, LIV/4 (Winter 1995), pp. 917–31

'Balkanize, v', http://dictionary.oed.com, accessed 26 October 2015

Bancroft, Angus, *Roma and Gypsy-travellers in Europe* (Aldershot, 2005)

Barany, Zoltan, *The East European Gypsies* (Cambridge, 2002)

Bartók, Béla, 'Gipsy Music or Hungarian Music?', in *Béla Bartók Essays*, ed. Benjamin Suchoff (Lincoln, NE, 1992), pp. 206–23

—, 'The Bartók-Möller Polemical Interchange', in *Béla Bartók Studies in Ethnomusicology*, ed. Benjamin Suchoff (Lincoln, NE, 1992), pp. 142–57

—, 'On Hungarian Music', in *Béla Bartók Essays*, ed. Benjamin Suchoff (Lincoln, NE, 1992), pp. 301–3

Baumann, Max Peter, 'The Reflection of the Roma in European Art Music', *World of Music*, XXXVIII/1 (1996), pp. 95–138

Beissinger, Margaret H., *The Art of the Lăutar: The Epic Tradition of Romania* (New York, 1991)

—, 'Occupation and Ethnicity: Constructing Identity Among Professional Romani (Gypsy) Musicians in Romania', *Slavic Review*, LX/1 (Spring 2001), pp. 24–49

—, 'The Performance of "Oriental Music" in Contemporary Romania', in *Ethnic Identities in Dynamic Perspective*, ed. Sheila Salo and Csaba Prónai (Budapest, 2003), pp. 229–36

—, '*Muziă Orientală*: Identity and Popular Culture in Postcommunist Romania', in *Balkan Popular Culture and the Ottoman Ecumene*, ed. Donna A. Buchanan (Lanham, MD, 2007), pp. 95–141

Bellman, Jonathan, 'Toward a Lexicon for the *Style Hongrois*', *Journal of Musicology*, IX/2 (Spring 1991), pp. 214–37

Bhopal, Kalwant, and Martin Myers, *Insiders, Outsiders and Others: Gypsies and Identity* (Hatfield, 2008)

Bideleux, Robert, and Ian Jeffries, *The Balkans: A Post-communist History* (Abingdon, 2007)

'Boban and Marko Marković Orchestra vs Fanfare Ciocărlia', www.asphalt-tango.de, accessed 26 October 2015

Borrow, George, *The Zincali* (London, 1841)

—, *The Bible in Spain* (London, 1843)

—, *Lavengro* [1851] (New York, 1991)

'A Brief History of Gogol Bordello', www.gogolbordello.com, accessed 10 July 2012

Brontë, Emily, *Wuthering Heights* [1847] (Harmondsworth, 1980)

Brown, Andrew, 'Introduction', in Prosper Mérimée, *Carmen* (London, 2004)

Brown, Julie, 'Bartók, the Gypsies and Hybridity in Music', in *Western Music and its Others*, ed. Georgia Born and David Hesmondhalgh (Berkeley, CA, 2000), pp. 119–42

Cartwright, Garth, 'Obituary: Nicolae Neacsu: Romanian Gypsy Violinist Who Conquered the West', *The Guardian* (16 September 2002), p. 20

—, 'Blowing Up a Storm', *The Independent* (5 May 2006), Arts and Book Review, p. 3

—, *Princes Amongst Men: Journeys with Gypsy Musicians* (London, 2005)

Cervantes Saavedra, Miguel de, *La Gitanilla*, trans. John Ozell (London, 1709)

Cilauro, Santo, Tom Gleisner and Rob Sitch, *Molvanîa: A Land Untouched by Modern Dentistry* (London, 2003)

Colmeiro, José F., 'Exorcising Orientalism: *Carmen* and the Construction of Oriental Spain', *Comparative Literature*, LIV/2 (Spring 2002), pp. 127–44

Crowe, David, 'The Gypsy Historical Experience in Romania', in *The Gypsies of Eastern Europe*, ed. David Crowe and John Kolsti (London, 1991), pp. 61–79

Cviic, Christopher, *Remaking the Balkans* (London, 1991)

Dregni, Michael, *Django: The Life and Music of a Gypsy Legend* (Oxford, 2004)

Finkielkraut, Alain, 'L'imposture Kusturica', *Le Monde* (2 June 1995), p. 16

'Flamenco', www.unesco.org, accessed 26 October 2015

Fonseca, Isabel, *Bury Me Standing: The Gypsies and Their Journey* (London, 1995)

'France Sends Roma Gypsies back to Romania', news.bbc.co.uk, 20 August 2010

Fraser, Angus, *The Gypsies* (Oxford, 1992)

Frith, Simon, 'Towards an Aesthetic of Popular Music', in *Music and Society: The Politics of Composition, Performance and Reception*, ed. Richard Leppert and Susan McClary (Cambridge, 1987), pp. 133–49

—, 'The Discourse of World Music', in *Western Music and Its Others*, ed. Georgina Born and David Hesmondhalgh (Berkeley, CA, 2000), pp. 305–22

Fry, Andy, *Paris Blues: African American Music and French Popular Culture* (Chicago, IL, 2014)

Garisto, Julie, 'Gogol Bordello's Eugene Hütz talks Gypsy Rock, Recording with Rick Rubin', http://blogs.tampabay.com, 23 July 2009

Givan, Benjamin, 'Django Reinhardt's Left Hand', in *Jazz Planet*, ed. E. Taylor Atkins (Jackson, MS, 2003), pp. 19–40

Glenny, Misha, *The Balkans* (London, 1999)

—, 'Only in the Balkans', *London Review of Books*, XXI/9 (29 April 1999), pp. 12–14.

Gocić, Goran, *Notes From the Underground: The Cinema of Emir Kusturica* (London, 2001)

Guglielmo, Rachel, and Timothy Waters, *Rights Denied: The Roma of Hungary* (New York, 1996)

Guilbault, Jocelyne, 'On Redefining the "Local" Through World Music', in *Ethnomusicology: A Contemporary Reader*, ed. Jennifer C. Post (New York, 2006), pp. 137–46

Hancock, Ian, *The Pariah Syndrome* (Ann Arbor, MI, 1987)

—, 'Origins of the Romani People', www.reocities.com, 17 April 1999

—, *We Are the Romani People* (Hatfield, 2002)

Hawes, Derek, and Barbara Perez, *The Gypsy and the State: The Ethnic Cleansing of British Society* (Bristol, 1995)

Hendrix, Jimi, *Starting at Zero: His Own Story* (London, 2013)

Heuwekemeijer, Julia, 'Taraf de Haïdouks as Re-gypsyfiers: A Critique on the Seductions of Authenticity', http://culturalmusicology.org, accessed 26 October 2015

Holroyd, Michael, *Augustus John* (London, 1996)

Hooker, Lynn M., *Redefining Hungarian Music from Liszt to Bartók* (Oxford, 2013)

Horne, Brian A., 'The Bards of Magnitizdat', in *Samizdat, Tamizdat, and Beyond*, ed. Friederike Kind-Kovacs and Jessie Labov (New York, 2013), pp. 175–89

Houghton-Walker, Sarah, *Representations of the Gypsy in the Romantic Period* (Oxford, 2014)

Howard-Flanders, William, *Balkania* (London, 1909)

Huq, Rupa, *Beyond Subculture* (London, 2006)

Iordanova, Dina, *Emir Kusuturica* (London, 2002)

Krasteva, Yonka, 'Western Writing and the (Re)Construction of the Balkans After 1989: The Bulgarian Case', in *The Balkans and the West*, ed. Andrew Hammond (Oxford, 2004), pp. 97–109

Kulish, Nicholas, 'As Economic Turmoil Mounts, So Do Deadly Attacks on Hungary's Gypsies', *New York Times* (26 April 2009), p. A1

Kuprin, Alexander, 'On the Passing of the Gypsy Song in Russia', *Lotus Magazine*,
viii/9 (June 1917), pp. 407–10

Lally, Conor, 'Gardaí Say More Roma in Line to be Deported', *Irish Times*
(17 August 2007), p. 4

Lange, Barbara Rose, '"What Was That Conquering Magic . . .": The Power
of Discontinuity in Hungarian Gypsy Nóta', *Ethnomusicology*, xli/3
(Autumn 1997), pp. 517–37

Leblon, Bernard, *Gypsies and Flamenco: The Emergence of the Art of Flamenco in
Andalusia* (Hatfield, 2000)

Lee, Ronald, 'A New Look at our Romani Origins and Diaspora', www.kopachi.
com, 2009

Lemon, Alaina, 'Hot Blood and Black Pearls: Socialism, Society, and Authenticity
at the Moscow Teatr Romen', *Theatre Journal*, xlviii/4 (December 1996),
pp. 479–94

—, 'Roma (Gypsies) in the ussr and the Moscow Teatr "Romen"', in *Gypsies:
An Interdisciplinary Reader*, ed. Diane Tong (New York, 1998), pp. 147–66

—, *Between Two Fires* (Durham, nc, 2000)

Lewis, Aidan, 'Italy Torn by Racial Strains', news.bbc.co.uk, 4 February 2009

Liszt, Franz, *The Gipsy in Music*, trans. Edwin Evans (London, 1926)

Lloyd, A. L., 'The Music of Rumanian Gypsies', *Proceedings of the Royal Musical
Association*, xc (1963–4), pp. 15–26

Lorca, Federico García, 'Play and Theory of the Duende', in *In Search of Duende*,
ed. and trans. Christopher Maurer (New York, 1998), pp. 48–62

—, *Selected Poems* (London, 1997)

Loya, Shay, *Liszt's Transcultural Modernism and the Hungarian-gypsy Tradition*
(Rochester, ny, 2011)

Lynskey, Dorian, 'There is No Such Thing as Gypsy Music', *The Guardian*
(24 November 2006), Features, p. 5

'Mahala Rai Banda', www.asphalt-tango.de, accessed 26 October 2015

'Making Human Rights for Roma a Reality', www.coe.int, 19 October 2015

Malvinni, David, *The Gypsy Caravan: From Real Roma to Imaginary Gypsies in
Western Music and Film* (New York, 2004)

Manuel, Peter, 'Andalusian, Gypsy, and Class Identity in the Contemporary
Flamenco Complex', *Ethnomusicology*, xxxiii/1 (Winter 1993), pp. 47–65

Margalit, Gilad, *Germany and its Gypsies* (Madison, wi, 2002)

Mariushiakova, Elena, and Vesselin Popov, 'The Roma – A Nation Without
a State? Historical Background and Contemporary Tendencies', in
Nationalisms Across the Globe: An Overview of Nationalisms in State-endowed

and Stateless Nations, ed. Wojciech J. Burszta, Tomasz Kamusella and
Sebastian Wojciechowski (Poznan, 2005), pp. 433–55

Matras, Yaron, *I Met Lucky People: The Story of the Romani Gypsies* (London, 2014)

Mazower, Mark, *The Balkans* (London, 2000)

Mérimée, Prosper, *Romans et Nouvelles*, vol. II (Paris, 1967)

Mitchell, Timothy, *Flamenco Deep Song* (New Haven, CT, 1994)

Mosora, Cristina, 'Manele the New Balkan Reggaeton', www.bridge-mag.com,
accessed 10 July 2012

Nickson, Chris, 'Taraf de Haïdouks', http://worldmusic.nationalgeographic.
com, accessed 10 July 2012

O'Keeffe, Brigid, *New Soviet Gypsies: Nationality, Performance, and Selfhood in the
Early Soviet Union* (Toronto, 2013)

Okely, Judith, *The Traveller-gypsies* (Cambridge, 1983)

Panassié, Hugues, *The Real Jazz*, trans. Anne Sorelle Williams (New York, 1942)

Pareles, Jon, 'The Whole World Gets Into the Groove', *New York Times*
(14 January 2014), p. C1

Pohren, D. E., *The Art of Flamenco* (Sevilla, 1967)

Port, Mattijs van de, 'Outstanding Musicians and the Stranger Within: Reflections
on Serb Perceptions of Gypsy Music', *Etnofoor*, X/1 (1997), pp. 7–27

—, 'The Articulation of Soul: Gypsy Musicians and the Serbian Other', *Popular
Music*, XXVIII/3 (1999), pp. 291–307

Porter, Hugh, 'Immigrant Punk: Eugene Hütz', www.time.com, 13 August 2008

Pushkin, Alexander, *The Gypsies* [1827], trans. Antony Wood (London, 2006)

Quintana, Bertha B., '"The Duende Roams Freely This Night": An Analysis of an
Interethnic Event in Granada, Spain', in *Gypsies: An Interdisciplinary Reader*,
ed. Diane Tong (New York, 1998), pp. 167–71

Raussert, Wilfred, 'Introduction: Traveling Sounds: Music, Migration and Identity
Formation', in *Traveling Sounds: Music, Migration and Identity in the U.S. and
Beyond*, ed. Wilfred Raussert and John Miller Jones (Berlin, 2008), pp. 9–21

Reynolds, Mark, 'Gypsy in £3m Benefit Fiddle', *Daily Express* (27 July 2010), p. 1

'Robert Soko: Biography', www.piranha.de, accessed 26 October 2015

Rorke, Bernard, and Orhan Usein, ed., *A Lost Decade: Reflections on Roma Inclusion
2005–2015* (Budapest, 2015)

'A Round with Gogol Bordello's Eugene Hütz', *Q Magazine* (April 2008), p. 30

Said, Edward W., *Orientalism* [1978] (London, 2003)

Sárosi, Bálint, *Gypsy Music*, trans. Fred Macnicol (Budapest, 1978)

Silverman, Carol, 'Music and Power: Gender and Performance Among Roma
(Gypsies) of Skopje, Macedonia', *World of Music*, XXXVIII/1 (1996), pp. 63–76

—, 'Rom (Gypsy) Music', in *The Garland Encyclopedia of World Music*, vol. VIII: *Europe*, ed. Timothy Rice, James Porter and Chris Goertzen (New York, 2000), pp. 270–93

—, 'Trafficking in the Exotic with "Gypsy" Music: Balkan Roma, Cosmopolitanism, and "World Music" Festivals', in *Balkan Popular Culture and the Ottoman Ecumene*, ed. Donna A. Buchanan (Lanham, MD, 2007), pp. 335–61

—, *Romani Routes: Cultural Politics and Balkan Music in Diaspora* (Oxford, 2012)

Stanton Smith, Gerald, *Songs to Seven Strings: Russian Guitar Poetry and Soviet Mass Song* (Bloomington, IN, 1984)

Stevenson, Rachel, 'Dale Farm Travellers: We Won't Just Get Up and Leave', *The Guardian* (27 July 2010), G2, p. 13

Stokes, Martin, 'Music and the Global Order', *Annual Review of Anthropology*, XXXIII (2004), pp. 47–72

—, 'Shedding Light on the Balkans: Sezen Aksu's Anatolian Pop', in *Balkan Popular Culture and the Ottoman Ecumene*, ed. Donna A. Buchanan (Lanham, MD, 2007), pp. 309–44

Szeman, Ioana, '"Gypsy Music" and Deejays: Orientalism, Balkanism and Romani Musicians', *TDR: The Drama Review*, LIII/3 (Autumn 2009), pp. 98–116

Taylor, Becky, *Another Darkness, Another Dawn: A History of Gypsies, Roma and Travellers* (London, 2014)

Timofeyev, Oleg, 'The Golden Age of the Russian Guitar: Repertoire, Performance Practice, and Social Function of the Russian Seven-string Guitar Music, 1800–1850', PhD thesis, Duke University, 1999

Timofeyev, Oleg, and Marco Bazzotti, 'The Seven-string Guitar in 19th-century Russian Culture', *Il Fronimo*, CIII (1998), pp. 27–40

Todorova, Maria, *Imagining the Balkans* (Oxford, 1997)

Traynor, Ian, 'Apartheid in the Heart of Europe: How Roma Children Lose Out on Education', *The Guardian* (16 November 2007), p. 25

Trumpener, Katie, 'The Time of the Gypsies: A "People without History" in the Narratives of the West', *Critical Inquiry*, XVIII/4 (1992), pp. 843–84

Udvardyova, Lucia, 'Eastern Haze: December 2013', www.electronicbeats.net, accessed 26 October 2015

Washabaugh, William, *Flamenco Music and National Identity in Spain* (Farnham, 2012)

Whyton, Tony, *Jazz Icons* (Cambridge, 2010)

Willems, Wim, *In Search of the True Gypsy*, trans. Don Bloch (London, 1997)

Wittgenstein, Ludwig, *Philosophical Investigations*, trans. G.E.M. Anscombe
  (Oxford, 1963)
Woods Peiró, Eva, *White Gypsies: Race and Stardom in Spanish Musicals*
  (Minneapolis, MN, 2012)
Žižek, Slavoj, '"You May!"', *London Review of Books*, XXI/6 (18 March 1999),
  pp. 3–6

DISCOGRAPHY

Aksu, Sezen, *Düğün ve Cenaze* (Universal, 1997)

Bajramović, Šaban, *Parno Gras* (Juvekomerc, 1997)

Bartók, Béla, *Mikrokosmos* (Naxos, 2006)

—, *A Portrait* (Naxos, 2007)

—, *Voices from the Past: Béla Bartók's 44 Duos and Original Field Recordings* (Tantara, 2014)

Basement Jaxx, 'Hey U' (Atlantic Jaxx, 2007)

Bizet, Georges, *Carmen* (Decca, 1985)

Boban Marković Orkestar, *Boban I Marko* (Piranha, 2003)

Boban and Marko Marković Orchestra vs Fanfare Ciocărlia, *Balkan Brass Battle* (Asphalt Tango, 2011)

Bregović, Goran, *Les Temps des Gitans* (Polygram, 1990)

—, *Music Inspired and Taken from Underground* (Mercury, 1995)

—, *Tales and Songs from Weddings and Funerals* (Mercury, 2002)

—, *Champagne for Gypsies* (Mercury, 2012)

Buttler, Ljiljana, and Mostar Sevdah Reunion, *The Mother of Gypsy Soul* (Snail Records, 2002)

Csókolom, *May I Kiss Your Hand* (Arhoolie Records, 1998)

De Lucía, Paco, *Plays Manuel de Falla* (Philips, 1978)

El Camarón de la Isla and Paco de Lucía, *El Camarón de la Isla con la Colaboración Especial de Paco de Lucía* (Philips, 1970)

Fanfare Ciocărlia, *Radio Paşcani* (Piranha, 1998)

—, *Gili Garabi* (Asphalt Tango, 2005)

—, *Queens and Kings* (Asphalt Tango, 2007)

Fanfare Ciocărlia and Adrian Raso, *Devil's Tale* (Asphalt Tango, 2014)

Galich, Aleksandr, *Когда Я Вернусь . . .* (Melodiya, 1989)

Gipsy Kings, *Greatest Hits* (Columbia, 1994)

Gogol Bordello, *Gypsy Punks: Underdog World Strike* (SideOneDummy, 2005)

—, *Trans-continental Hustle* (American Recordings, 2010)

Grappelli, Stéphane, *Homage to Django* (Classic Jazz, 1972)

Grisman, David, *Hot Dawg* (Horizon, 1979)

Hendrix, Jimi, *Band of Gypsys* (Capitol, 1970)

J.U.F., *Gogol Bordello vs Tamir Muskat* (Stinky, 2004)

Kal, *Kal* (Asphalt Tango, 2006)

Kalyi Jag, *Fekete Tüz / Black Fire – Gypsy Folk Songs from Hungary*
(Hungaroton, 1988)

Koçani Orkestar, *Alone At My Wedding* (Crammed Discs, 2006)

Kolpakov Trio, *Rodava Tut* (Opre, 1995)

Kusturica, Emir, and the No Smoking Orchestra, *Bande Originale du Filme:
Chat Noir Chat Blanc* (Barclay, 2000)

—, *Unza Unza Time* (Universal, 2003)

—, *Emir Kusturica's Time of the Gypsies* (Decca, 2007)

Lagrène, Biréli, *My Favorite Django* (Dreyfus Jazz, 1995)

Liszt, Franz, *Complete Hungarian Rhapsodies* (Philips, 2004)

Mahala Raï Banda, *Mahala Raï Banda* (Crammed Discs, 2004)

—, *Ghetto Blasters* (Asphalt Tango, 2009)

Minune, Adrian Copilul, *Inestimabil* (Autentic Music, 2006)

Okudzhava, Bulat, *Песни (Стихи И Музыка)* (Melodiya, 1976)

Redžepova, Esma, *Chaje Shukarije* (World Connection, 2000)

Reinhardt, Django, and the Quintet of the Hot Club of France with Stéphane
Grappelli, *Djangology* (RCA Victor, 1961)

Shantel, *Disko Partizani* (Crammed Discs, 2007)

—, *Planet Paprika* (Crammed Discs, 2009)

Slavic Soul Party, *Bigger* (Barbès Records, 2005)

Szabó, Gábor, *Spellbinder* (Impulse!, 1966)

Talisman, *A Tribute to Stesha the Russian-gypsy Diva: Early Music of Russian Gypsies*
(Naxos, 2005)

Taraf de Haïdouks, *Band of Gypsies* (Crammed Discs, 2001)

—, *Maskarada* (Crammed Discs, 2007)

—, *Band of Gypsies 2* (Crammed Discs, 2011)

—, *Of Lovers, Gamblers and Parachute Skirts* (Crammed Discs, 2015)

Taraf of Clejani [Taraf de Haïdouks], *Roumanie – Musique des Tziganes de
Walachie – Les lăutari de Clejani* (Ocora, 1988)

Timofeyev, Oleg, and John Schneiderman, *The Russian Guitar 1800–1850* (Brilliant
Classics, 2016)

Trans-Siberian March Band, *The Tractor Makers' Ball* (self-released, 2010)

Various Artists, *Artists of the Gipsy Theatre 'Romen'* (Melodiya, 1969)

—, *Balkan Beats* (Eastblok, 2006)

—, *Robert Soko Balkan Beats Soundlab* (Piranha, 2012)

Via Romen, *My Two Homes* (self-released, 2010)

Vysotsky, Vladimir, *Владимир Высоцкий Поет Свои Песни* (Melodiya, 1978)

ACKNOWLEDGEMENTS

This book has its origins in a project on gypsy punk undertaken at the London Consortium, and I'm grateful to have had the opportunity to be part of a unique PhD programme, and for the wide-ranging interest and advice of its staff and students. I had excellent supervision: many thanks are due to Steve Connor for his enthusiasm for the project and his polymathic advice, and to Ioana Szeman for her valuable expertise and ability to tease out threads of argument from tangled text. I'm also grateful to Carol Silverman and Martin Stokes for insights and suggestions that led me to think more widely around gypsy punk and other forms of gypsy music.

I thank John Scanlan for his initial interest in the book project and his suggestions on how to develop its scope and draw its parameters. Thanks also to Michael Leaman, Harry Gilonis and Jess Chandler at Reaktion Books for their careful and supportive work refining the unpolished text, tracking down images and turning the manuscript into the finished book.

Gogol Bordello enter towards the end of this book, but they were in fact my way into gypsy music. I am fortunate that the band allowed themselves to be so accessible, and thank them for being happy to talk about their work, and the work of other musicians; for sharing their riders; and for throwing magnificent after-parties. The Gogol Bordello online forum, Avenue-B, has been a hugely valuable resource for its intelligent debates not only about gypsy punk but about gypsy music more widely. I am indebted to its creator, Alison Clarke, and to many of its insightful contributors.

Finally, I thank my family for their ongoing support and belief in me, and thank Merinne Whitton for her advice, patience and love.

PHOTO ACKNOWLEDGEMENTS

The author and publishers wish to express their thanks to the following sources of illustrative material and / or permission to reproduce it. Some locations are also supplied here for reasons of brevity.

Photo Alamy Stock Photo: p. 64; photos courtesy the author: pp. 39, 79, 80, 183; photo Emilio Beauchy: p. 139; photo Bundesarchiv: p. 30; photo John Coulter: p. 42; photo Dejan Ćirić Websites (www.guca.rs): p. 102; Dulwich Picture Gallery, London: p. 24; photo Angela Filigenzi, reproduced courtesy Matthew Grasso: p. 129; photo Fota Akbaba: p. 179; Peter Hermes Furian / Alamy Stock Photo: p. 12; Global Music Enterprises: p. 117; reproduced by kind permission of Michael Hirsh and Hardie Grant Books, South Yarra, Victoria, Australia: p. 89; © and reproduced courtesy Stefano Kappel and BalkanBeats: p. 172; Library of Congress, Washington, DC (William P. Gottlieb Collection): p. 155; photo Michael Mann (c / o Piranha Records): p. 103; photos Danilo Moroni / Alamy Live News: pp. 106, 109; National Portrait Gallery, London: p. 21; reproduced courtesy Christina Oswald / guilty76 artist management: p. 173; private collection: p. 57; photo Reuters / Zoubeir Souissi: p. 51; photos Sputnik / Alamy Stock Photo: pp. 122, 130; photo Björn Steinz: p. 33; photo Carlos Teixidor Cadenas: p. 139; photos ZUMA / Alamy Stock Photo: pp. 77, 112.

Dennis Jarvis, the copyright holder of the image on p. 53, has published it online under conditions imposed by a Creative Commons Attribution-Share Alike 2.0 Generic license; Thomas Goller, the copyright holder of the image on p. 57 (reproduced by permission of the Family May-Weissheimer and Thomas Goller), has published it online under conditions imposed by a Creative Commons Attribution-Share Alike 2.5 Generic license; and Estevoaei at Galician Wikipedia, the copyright holder of the image on p. 97, has published it online under conditions imposed by a Creative Commons Attribution-Share Alike 3.0

Unported license. Readers are free to share – to copy, distribute and transmit these images alone; to remix – to adapt these images alone; under the following conditions: attribution – readers must attribute either image in the manner specified by the author(s) or licensor(s) but not in any way that suggests that these parties endorse them or their use of the work(s), and share alike – if readers alter, transform, or build upon this image, they may distribute the resulting work only under the same or similar license to this one.

INDEX